Dedicated to all
Ballinascreen
Publicans
Poitín-makers
and Poets
of the Past
Present
and Future

Ballinascreen Historical Society, 2013

I.S.B.N. 978-0-9575255-0-4

Screen Spirit

Pubs, Poteen & Poetry in Ballinascreen

by the

barowners
bartenders
barmaids
barkeeps
barmen
barflies
barred
and
bards
of
Ballinascreen

compiled and edited
by a barking mad Strawdog
Frank Kelly

Publisher's Preface

Frank Kelly, in a trans-Atlantic letter from Canada in March 2002, mentioned *an idea which won't go away. Why not a book on The Bars of Ballinascreen? History, anecdotes, poems, songs, photos, drawings, etc.* His inspiration had come from "Johnny Paul" Kelly's poem entitled "Paul Johnnie" which had appeared in Ballinascreen Historical Society's first publication – "The Wee Black Tin" – in 1980. Frank had just completed what he describes as a "self-published family-history project" and, having quoted Johnny Paul's verses in it, wondered *was this the only poem celebrating the pubs of Ballinascreen?*

In the intervening years Frank produced two very attractive, short-run, draft editions of "Screen Spirit" for private circulation amongst family and friends. As historical details of long-gone public houses accumulated and Frank's talent as a story-teller, poet and general word-smith seemed to grow exponentially, the committee of Ballinascreen Historical Society felt it would be a major coup if this long-time Straw exile would give us permission to publish his work. Our request was positively received and now this very fine cocktail of fact and fiction, so liberally sprinkled with humour and clever innuendo, is in general circulation. The Society has a long publishing pedigree and this takes us in a more light-hearted direction, but we are extremely proud of this book which Frank has now produced.

Frank's literary output now follows in the long Ballinascreen bardic tradition stretching, in more modern times, from David Hepburn of Drumard to John "Paul" Kelly of Doon and Geordie Barnett of Owenreagh, together with many other unpublished scribes. The Society is deeply, deeply grateful to him for generously shaping and honing this literary work and presenting it to us ready for publication.

In his introduction the author mentions *the damage excessive alcohol consumption is capable of doing to otherwise sane, decent, healthy people* and so the publisher, Ballinascreen Historical Society, needs to state that the Society does not necessarily endorse any views expressed within these pages.

Having included this clause so that the Society is not seen to be promoting a culture which some might see as distasteful, we encourage the reader to wallow in nostalgia for people and places long since gone and to take each verse of "Cú Chulainn's Crawl" slowly, analysing the clever references and appreciating the sharp humour which gleams here and there.
Thank you, Frank.

Ballinascreen Historical Society
C/o 5 Tobermore Road
Draperstown
BT45 7AG

> To search the public houses,
> Of the village one and all
> He started down at Thomas Quinn's,
> To give him the first call ...

Introduction

The idea of a book about drinking, pubs, poitín-making and poetry in Ballinascreen has been around ever since local bard, "Johnny Paul" Kelly's 1930's poem *Paul Johnnie* (quoted above) crawled its way into this partly pickled brain some dozen years ago, so it seemed inevitable that a tour of that proud parish's relationship to drink would find its way into words and pictures. Many of the excellent non-fiction books that have been produced about Ballinascreen by local people have been about the churches, graveyards, schools, and family histories of that parish, with little attention given to what many consider an unwholesome, unholy even, dark side of the community ... its pubs. This is understandable given the damage excessive alcohol consumption is capable of doing to otherwise sane, decent, healthy people but it would be unfortunate if we lost the lore of drink and drinking establishments *which are disappearing fast* and which, whether we like it or not, have played such a large part in the history of Ballinascreen.

This book is not some kind of Ryan, Murphy or Cloyne report on drinking in Ballinascreen, nor is it a glorification of drink and pubs. It's just a bit of a lightly-researched 'crawl' through the sparsely documented history but abundant lore of an aspect of Ballinascreen for which it has long been quite famous, if not notorious. It makes no claims to be a serious social study or even accurate history and, although there are plenty of factual accounts and statistics scattered throughout, it barely scratches the surface of the lore that's out there. A bit of embellishment here and there has to be expected, given the nature of the subject.

Acknowledgements go to all the publicans, past and present, who contributed facts *and* fiction, especially to the late Joseph McAllister who was very much alive when all this started. Thanks also to publicans, Gerry and Peter McAllister, John Joe Bradley, Michael & Colin Doyle, Charlie McNally, Theresa & Christine Fullen, Deirdre & Barney McAuley, Tracey McAlary and to Maurice Regan who kindly drove me home after a 'forgotten' night of 'research' in his premises. Others who helped (but don't "necessarily endorse"!) with inspiration, stories and photos were Anne McAllister, "A MacGabhann", James Vallely, "A Strawman"; Kevin Kelly and Randy McNaught (for computer help), Paul Regan, Matt Regan, Steven Noonan, Shane Kelly, Mickey Kelly, Bernie Kelly, Patsy McShane, Mary McKernan, Isabelle Hegarty, Frankie Hegarty, Jimmy Kennedy, Gerry Cochrane (dec. 2013), Paddy Gray, Joe Diamond, John & Jim "Jamie Mick" Kelly who propped me up on a bit of a 'research' crawl. Special thanks to the tireless historian and editor, Graham Mawhinney and the Ballinascreen Historical Society for generously and sportingly allowing this book to be published under its reputable name.

Numerous books helped to get and to keep this whole business going, some listed in the bibliography on page 168. Listening to the good *and bad* rhymes of Robert Service, Leonard Cohen and Bob Dylan helped a bit too. Respectful toasts to the late Nora Ní Chathain, my "Aunt Ellie" Kelly, Seamus Heaney and Brendan Kelly for instilling an interest in Irish myth, verse and art. (The wee man at the foot of this and many other pages was my brother Brendan's 'trademark'). Finally, many thanks to my wife Rosaleen for putting up with all this, especially over the last five years.

Frank Kelly, Samhain, 2013

Ancient Pubs in Ballinascreen
Portals for potions, porter and poteen

Little is known about the ancient bars of the parish but that shouldn't deter us from devising a history of its public houses stretching back into the mists of time. The Tuatha de Danaan, that race of demigods who retreated to Tír na nÓg in the face of the warlike Milesians, our human Irish ancestors, are well known around Ballinascreen. They inhabit all corners of the parish and are seen by imaginative inebriates to this day, inebriates who have the good sense not to drink and drive but who wander the roads and loanin's on foot. Those who have been drinking porter at their local and go for a dander of an evening, see the Tuatha de Danaan as the aos sí, the fairies, flitting about on the siohs (their hidden domains) of Doon, Drumard or Dunlogan; those on the harder stuff see them as demi-gods arising above the hills of Comhrac, Cahore or Crockmore; those on more exotic modern cocktails or expensive European wines see them as a race of extra-terrestrials in their flying ships swooping in over Moyheelan, Moykeeran or Town Upper to abduct them and administer to them the Ideal Drink, the one that all drinkers long for, the one that makes them keep drinking, searching for that ultimate bar, that portal of the gods where the other-worldly Barman will serve them the perfect pint of porter that will transport them to Tír na nÓg as an enfeebled Fionn McCool was so transported when he passed through the fastnesses of Glenconkeyne many moons ago and stopped in at more than one of its many watering holes to lick his wounds, slake his thirst, regain his cool.

> *Feeble he drinks--the potion speeds*
> *Through every joint and pore;*
> *To palsied age fresh youth succeeds--*
> *Fionn, of the swift and slender steeds,*
> *Becomes himself once more.*
>
> from *The Chase* (old Irish poem)

You can't ask for a more refreshing drink than that.
From *The Book of Fermoy* more evidence of the central role of drink in this Irish netherworld where Manannan, the sea god, who seemed to be a kind of mythical tavern keeper:

> Manannán also gave each sidh the Fled Goibniu (Feast of Goibniu) and the Pigs of Manannán. The former are drinks, possibly ales, which keep the Tuatha De Danann young.

The keepers of this lore about the Tuatha were none other than the druids. For all their muddled mystery-laden reputation as holy men, lawmakers and teachers there is one undoubted fact about them; they were secretive. And who is to say that the secrets they most guarded weren't those of the brewing and/or distribution of those ales and potions that transported drinkers to the gates of Tír na nÓg?

"The Giant's Grave" in Ballybriest near Corick, a possible site for a

Fulacht Fiadh?

Back in the 1950s archaeologist M. J. O'Kelly was the first to identify fulachta fiadh ("wild pits"), sites thought to be neolithic cooking pits near sources of water and fuel for fires, found all over Ireland but especially in Co. Cork (2000 out of 4500 nationwide!). Two modern-day archaeologists (and beer lovers), Billy Quinn and Declan Moore have argued that these pits like the one (below) in Drombeg, Cork, were not just for cooking food but for brewing beer, the long central troughs filled with water and grain into which red hot rocks were dropped to heat the mixture and begin the fermentation process. For more information on the Quinn/Moore "Moore Group" discoveries and brewing experiments see http://www.mooregroup.ie/beer/fulacht.html.

The "portal" structures found around or near these fulachta fiadh do not look unlike the chambered grave stones of Ballybriest (above) or what may have been near the burial pits in Bolia, Ballinascreen before they were removed by archaeologists from NI Environment Agency in 2008 or so, to make way for "progress", the ever-expanding gravel quarry which is eating its way through the hills close to that spiritual "source of water", Lough Patrick. Here we have a close, not necessarily comfortable or respectable association, between burial sites and drink-making, to say nothing of druids and places of worship, an association which will crop up with some frequency in the course of our travels in Ballinascreen. To be honest, no fulachta fiadh have been positively identified around the parish but that might be explained by its long, venerable history of successfully screening such secretive sites from excise men, archaeologists and other nosey people. As far as more recent burial sites are concerned (Ballinascreen church graveyards) you will find almost every one of them in close proximity to a pub that was once a "spirit grocer's".

The Druids of Draperstown?

100% proof in the spelling

Druids and druidesses have always been associated with those mysterious man-made neolithic mounds (sıohs mhonaraıche) like Newgrange and the many so-called chambered graves around Ballinascreen. What has not been associated with the druids themselves until now, is their role in "the drink". They made potions which had the same effect as those given to Finn McCool and Cú Chulainn. It is now clear that those great archaeological treasures were not just burial mounds but the very portals of Tír na nÓg ... neolithic spirit houses where the druids distilled and distributed youth-giving potions. How do we know this? Here we are indebted to a Macalister, maybe a distant cousin of the McAllisters of Straw, owners of the bar beside the old graveyard there for 2 generations (and equally helpful in later stages of this history), the late R.A. Stewart Macalister, an Irish archaeologist who, among many achievements, wrote a book called *The Secret Languages of Ireland*.

Now, to be fair, Macalister never actually said that those mysterious artificial mounds of rock and soil were neolithic pubs; not in so many words, but all the evidence gleaned through years of painstaking etymological detective work by this editor, using Macalister's glossaries, while under the influence of certain inspirational potions, has led to this groundbreaking conclusion. Not only that, but as we shall see, many of the words that Macalister unearthed, which he traces back directly to druidic language, have now been found to have strong connections to Ballinascreen and its townlands, making it the very *fons et origo*, the fount/source/spring and origin (we'll see this phrase used again in the 19th century with regards to the parish) of the making of mind-altering liquors and of the institutions of their distribution.

To not-so subtly slake the reader's druth for the ensuing erudition, let us look at the name of the present day town that is the commercial hub of Ballinascreen. It is widely accepted that it was named after the planters' Worshipful Company of Drapers of London who developed it and gave it such wide streets and a fine courthouse where all those native illicit distillers could be prosecuted, but why did the majority native population acquiesce so readily to this very Anglo name? When you consider that the far more loyal planter town of Tobermore, right next door to Draperstown, kept its old Gaelic name, well, why was there not a campaign in Ballinascreen to have the same privilege? Why is there no record of ruckus, rebellion or riot over this? Macalister provides the answer. One of the secret languages derived from ancient druidic languages is Shelta, the original Shelta (not the modern "Cant" version) mostly spoken by a few hard-to-find travellers at the time, in the 1930's, when Macalister was frequenting taverns in places like Liverpool with large Irish immigrant populations, while he searched for those secret languages.

Baile Na Buideal

It was in the secret language of these "outsiders" who were often involved in activities which needed to be shaded from "the law" that Macalister found the links to the ancient bardic tradition which had been suppressed and marginalized by the same law. From the secret languages of the bards he was led to the druidic tradition itself and to Ogham. But let us not get ahead of ourselves. In that secret Shelta language the word for "bottle" is *driper* or *dreeper*. It doesn't take much of a scholar to see where this is going. No wonder there was little protest in the parish when the planters settled on the name Draperstown. No wonder the majority native population with its old, Gaelic, bardic, druidic collective consciousness or unconsciousness even, accepted the new name without a fight. It was 19th century inadvertent advertising. Product placement. And, far from arousing the ire of the locals, it must have cheered them. They surely celebrated yet another getting-one-over on their rulers with some renewed, spirited distilling, selling and supping as it became firmly entrenched in the mind of the rest of mid-Ulster that *Driperstown* was *the* place to find the real thing.

And "Ballinascreen" itself? To cast any doubt on the origins of that name is nigh on blasphemy but we must risk being struck down here and go deep. Certainly in "modern" Irish scrín means "shrine" and that religious meaning was bate into us from an early age but in the more anciently rooted language of Shelta *skrin* or *skreen* means "counterfeit". Even without resorting to that *revealing* Shelta meaning, 'screen' is a covert word. It may have been a screen set up to hide the priest saying mass in Penal days but a screen can hide many things that need to be kept from prying eyes or ears, not least the making of potions or poteens. Ireland and particularly Ballinascreen has long been known for not saying what it means, saying plenty but saying little, hiding its true colours, deception, obfuscation, circumspection, screening its culture from outside threats with crafty, coded communication, wily winks and nods. "What ever you say, say nothing."

You could take all the townland names of Ballinascreen and find similar old meanings that point to a culture steeped in the mysterious world of moonshine, money and mead but we're not in the mood at the moment to maunder on about the meanings of Moneyneena, Moneyconey, or Moneyquiggy. We have to go to the source for the true spirit of Ballinascreen ... Ogham, the most secretive, loaded language of the lot, a language created by Ogma the Gaulish-Celtic deity shown on the left. Ogma was also known in ancient Greek culture as Ogmios, an older, wiser, more refined personification of Heracles or Hercules, he of the twelve labours.

Moyard Mountain Dew
High Times in the Sperrins

Ogham, the language created by Ogma or Ogmios (depicted on previous page) the ancient Celtic deity of eloquence and poetry, powerfully associated with the lapping of liquours to loosen the lips. There are numerous townlands in Ballinascreen with links to Ogma, Ogmios and Ogham but don't expect any easy ones. We are still dealing with the secret and the esoteric and it will take some stretching of words and symbols, to say nothing of belief, to fully plumb the depths of deception at work in Ogham. Whether it is originally a hand sign language, as Macalister believed, or simply the written sign language scored on rocks or whether there was a spoken tongue associated with it, it is always elusive, as can only be expected from a system of communication that sometimes dealt with the "black arts". As befits Ogma himself with all those precious metal chains hanging out of his mouth tied to the ears of his listeners, wordplay, anagrams, reversals, rhymes, puns, alliterations, illiterations, over-indulgent loquaciousness, speaking in tongues, tongues in cheeks, drink-talking, new-wine mumbling, slurred speech, drooling drivel and garbled gibberish all played a part in the origins and utterings of the names of the townlands and people in Ballinascreen and still do. The letters of Ogham have long been associated with the names of native Irish trees (especially The Oak) and wee bushes sacred to druidic practice and this important connection we will revisit later.

Glen-*gom(h)na* townland yields readily enough to anagram treatment (of *ogham* itself) so Glengomna may be a jumping-off point in our discoveries and in fact it is well known to this day as a source of the rare oul mountain dew. Even Fr. Patrick Heron, born and bred in Glengomna, and a Gaelic scholar, admitted that "gomna" could have many meanings, as is the case with all townland names. But first let's take a road less travelled to an even more productive locale, to the Sixtowns townland of Moyard where an archaeological find which has heretofore been a mystery will yield high returns as, plainly, its name, even in late Irish, also does. It was the stone quern (below) which was, at the time of the 1836 Ordnance Survey Memoir, in the home of Hugh Bradley of Moyard, possibly the same Bradleys who owned pubs around Ballinascreen 100 years later, including a Hughie Bradley who owned Miles's spirit grocery in Straw. The quern had been found in the Moyola and was at one time the bottom stone of a mill for grinding grain which of course is a necessary part of the process of making spirits not just flour. The strange markings on the stone have never been deciphered ... until now.

Page 34; 1836-7 Ordnance Survey (Ballinascreen)

Standing Stoned in the Sixtowns
Come to my Boozalum

There is a variation of Ogham, called "Fionn's Ladder" a kind of shorthand using, instead of the usual multiple strokes of basic Ogham set on a vertical line on most stones, a series of "flag" shapes here set on a circle instead. Firstly we need to straighten out the marks to the vertical "Fionn's Ladder" form and then, for the benefit of the modern reader, to the horizontal, which makes it look like this.

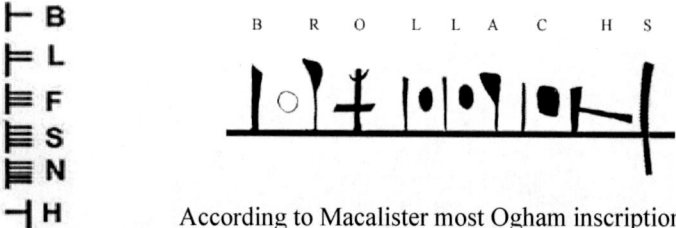

⊢	B
⊫	L
⊫	F
⊫	S
⊫	N
⊣	H
⊣	D
⫣	T
⫣	C
⫣	Q
✚	M
✚	G
✚	NG
✚	Z
✚	R
‖	P
╋	A
╪	O
╪	U
╪	E
╪	I
✳	EA
◇	OI
⌐⌐	UI
⋉	IA
⊞	AE

B   R   O   L   L   A   C   H   S

According to Macalister most Ogham inscriptions were proper names of people. Using the key on the left but then converting it to the Fionn's Ladder "shorthand" form which is far too complicated for the average reader to follow here, unless under the influence, we find that this inscription is indeed a proper name ... *Brollach* which means "bosom" in Irish although the "R" is debatable and if omitted would leave us with ... a rather damning indictment of this whole enterprise? Leave the "R" in and we have the root word of the name *O'Brolchan, or O'Brollaghan,* which anglicizes to *Bradley* and since all the letters are on a bar (or roundtable?) it is obvious that we have here a very early, druidic era sign for a spirit seller's establishment. Its earlier use as a millstone is a perfect indicator, if it wasn't already obvious, for the ancient drinker, probably a weary, thirsty, semi-literate, shepherd, that he had reached his destination where the juice of the (ground) barley would flow. If the reader has any doubt about this "translation", he can wade his way through Macalister's book and check the intermediate steps but be warned, it would be similar to wading the Moyola in search of a stone you didn't know was there.

Why was this millstone in the Moyola? Was it thrown there to hide it and its message? Were there excise men in ancient Ireland? Was "Bradley's" tumbled by them at some stage and the sign dumped in the river? Was an early Bradley attached to the stone i.e. given the biblical punishment for selling spirits to minors, causing them to "stumble"?

Moyard is of course the only townland in the Sixtowns with a pub today, *The Shepherd's Res*t, one of the most remote bars in Ireland and one of the most popular and one we will take a good long look at later. Could this ancient millstone sign also be a sign that the Sixtowns not only had the earliest church in Ballinascreen but the earliest spirit seller too? Is it just coincidence that the owners of *The Shepherds Rest* before the Doyle family were Bradleys? It's almost certain that the Hugh Bradley who had the quern in his home knew rightly what the symbols on it meant and what its final use was but why would he tell some Dublin Castle surveyor trying to map and take inventory of every nook and crannog of his ancestral home, leaving no stone unturned?

An ancient Shepherds Rest?

For much of the ancient history of spirits in the Screen we are indebted to Macalister but also to a Kelly, another name, like the Bradleys and McAllisters, found countless times among the purveyors of potions in the parish. The earliest Kellys of Ballinascreen, mentioned in written records are the O'Kellys of An Chraobh, the townland of Crieve. John O'Donovan in one of his Ordnance Survey letters written in 1834 states that,

> *"The O'Kellys were the hereditary Seanchies of Gleann Concadhain. There is a tradition that Keating (Geoffrey Keating 1570 - 1644), visited O'Kelly when compiling his "History of Ireland". The Seanchie looked over the Doctor's book very carefully, but found that he had spoken very little about the noble families of Ulster, upon which he told the Doctor that he had favoured Munstermen and concealed the history of Ulster which was the most distinguished province in Ireland. He therefore refused to give Keating any information from the vast collection of Annals and other documents he had before him."*

What happened to those annals? Were they burned? Tradition has it that during the preparations for the 'stations' (when the priest would visit a home to say Mass) at a house somewhere in Ballinascreen (perhaps Crieve or Doon) old books, written in Gaelic, were found. A local schoolmaster, unversed in the native language, was of the opinion that the books contained information on the 'black arts' and that if the priest were to say Mass in the same house where these books were found that it would be a sacrilege. He ordered that the books be burned. It turned out that the books had been 'annals' containing valuable historical information about the parish ... perhaps those very annals so jealously guarded by the seanchie O'Kelly. A schoolmaster "ordered that the books be burned". But the idea that someone knew they were annals of historical significance, even after the burning, was suspicious.

The mystery remained ... until now. A few years ago, after this editor had compiled a history of the Kellys of Straw in which he bemoaned the loss of these annals, a Kelly of Bancran (near Crieve) whose full identity must be hidden to protect him/her from modern burning schoolmasters, found, in an old byre on his/her farm, some partly burnt vellum pages in a JACOBS biscuit tin under a pile of dried up cowdung. This Kelly had read "The Kellys of Straw" history so of course turned the vellum manuscript over to scholarly experts. It was written in Gaelic but liberally blended with other languages that only recently made sense ... Ogham, Shelta and Bog Latin. With the help of a reputable, though somewhat stocious Gaelic scholar and Macalister's secret language glossaries the fragmented text was loosely translated and sure enough that burning schoolmaster was found to have been right; the vellum pages did contain some "sacrilegeous black arts" ... recipes for the making of potent but potable potions that the (druidic?) scribe actually claimed would transport the drinker to "other dimensions" But these recipes are almost incidental because the bulk of the pages contain pieces of a long, rambling, doggerel epic (with similar looking verse shapes to a few verses in *The Táin)* about the coming of Cú Chulainn to Glenconkeyne for the purpose of recovering from his wounds before the final battle against Queen Medb and her 'southern' armies.

As you can see below, the manuscript is both complex and charred but as time goes on more and more of the burnt pages will yield up their secrets thanks to technological innovations and spirited, inspired invention.

Lebhor Cac na Bhó

The Annals of Crieve
or The Book of The Dung Cow

In *The Táin*, most of which was gleaned from the **Lebhor na hUidre** or *The Book of the Dun Cow*, there are long catalogues of names of warriors, and places, many of them untraceably obscure, but in the **Lebhor Cac na Bhó**, *The Book of the Dung Cow* (we will use this designation for the semi-burnt manuscript) Ballinascreen readers will see some very familiar names. But before we look in awe at this remarkable long-lost doggerel, let the tautly stretched belief of the reader be relaxed with some corroborating evidence for the obvious central tenet of the book itself, namely, that Cú Chulainn did in fact visit Ballinascreen. O'Donovan's 1836 survey notes include a paragraph about the derivation of Drumderg townland. O'Donovan did not believe all he heard from the crafty denizens of Drumderg but he did attach great importance to the way townland names had their origins in folk tales and legends ...

> *Darige Dawna Macadrille a foreign chief who came to fight some of the Irish Phoenicians is the giant buried in Drumderg where the ancient standing stones are on the verge of a stream and holding of Patrick Diamond. He was killed by* **Coocoolun** *[Cú Chulainn] and immediately buried in the aforesaid place, it being the site of the battle. The eminence was from that period called* **Drimadirig** *and gave its name to the townland though the name has subsequently changed and called Drumderg.*

Cú Chulainn Comes to The Screen

There is some doubt about the name of this "giant" "foreign chief". Oral tradition has it as **Darige Dawna Macadrille** but in the manuscript *her* name appears as **Duna Dirigean Mercmobille**. Before you enter the world of *Cú Chulainn's Crawl* you need the key (below) to Ogham symbols (written horizontally), their sounds in old Irish and the trees or plants associated with them. This key will unlock the names of druid "spirits" derived from those trees that grew in the townlands mentioned in the doggerel. There are many real places mentioned here and there may even be some real characters and real events depicted, pieces of history of drinking~in Ballinascreen, but if you wish to skip the rhyme and get on with the reason, turn to page 103.

SYMBOL	SOUND	NAME	TREE	SYMBOL	SOUND	NAME	TREE
ᛁ	b	Beith	birch		sw	Straif	blackthorn
ᛁᛁ	l	Luis	rowan		r	Ruis	elder
ᛁᛁᛁ	f	Fearn	alder		a	Ailm	fir, pine
ᛁᛁᛁᛁ	s	Sail	sally, willow		o	Onn	whin, gorse
ᛁᛁᛁᛁᛁ	n	Nion	ash		u	Ur	heather
	y	Uath	white-thorn		e	Eadhadh	aspen
	d	Dair	oak		i	Iodhadh	yew
	t	Tinne	holly		ea	Eabhadh	aspen
	k	Coll	hazel		oi	Or	ivy
	kw	Ceirt	oak, apple		ui	Uilleann	honeysuckle
	m	Muin	vine		ae	Eamancholl	hazel (twin)
	g	Gort	ivy		ia	Pin	gooseberry
	gw	nGeadal	fern				

Cú Chulainn's Crawl

> "After them the Tuatha De arrived
> Concealed in their dark clouds ..."
> from *The Book of Ballymote*

The illuminations accompanying the text are a combination of Ballinascreen landscapes and Tír na nÓg, that land that some say is far above and/or far to the west of Ireland, a new-found land that constantly shape-shifts and time-shifts, a fluid land that knows no national boundaries, a heavenly land but not a supernatural one, a land right in front of our noses or as Rupert Brooke once put it ...

> They say that the Dead die not, but remain
> Near to the rich heirs of their grief and mirth.
> I think they ride the calm mid-heaven, as these,
> In wise majestic melancholy train,
> And watch the moon, and the still-raging seas,
> And men, coming and going on the earth.

As all poetasters and poitín makers must, the ancient rhymer of *Cú Chulainn's Crawl* poured this first verse naggin libation in supping supplication to the muse, the Leanan Síohe. (pr. *lan*-awn shee) before embarking on this Drunkard's Walk.

> Sláinte maith O Leanan síohe
> Here's to amusin and abusin me
> Lip me and lap me with sips from your still
> Woo me and love me and free me at will
> Let the wooin brim over with words of delight
> Let the lovin be languid with rhythm that's tight
> Let the freedom be fulsome   your beauty on show
> So it's you that is heard   not someone we know.

Cú Chulainn's Crawl
in
Seven Drinking Days

1. Sliabh Gallon Draes
2. Sé Dhaile Taes
3. Cnoc Mór Craes
4. hÚdaigh's Uaes
5. Moyola Maes
6. Cross Fair Daes
7. Strag Dog Straes

1. Sliabh Gallon Braes

Cú Chulainn fought so often in the Táin
His wounds were thick from head to groin
He needed rest   this shattered hulk
To heal his bloody aechin bulk
A man of such prodigious feats
Needs fifty tons of farls and meats
But most of all he needs a drink
Says he to Laeg 'What do you think?
Where will we find the finest booze
To stanch the pain and gore I ooze?'

Now Laeg   his trusted charioteer
A man from Gleann Con Cadhain or near
Who knew mid-Uladh more than most
Had often raised a tankard toast
In far remotest Sperrin vales
Where all the finest spirits   ales
Distilled to pure exactitude
By dark druidic brotherhood (or sisterhood)
Were found in part of Gleann Con Cadhain
A verdant fastness called An Scrín.

Laeg drags his half-dead Boss's
Carcass on his chariot and hosses
He drives them hard   for all they're worth
Hell for leather   headin north
Through Ard Macha and Tír Eoghain

Until around Sliabh Gallon goin''
The way is blocked by one huge hound
That gave its name to all around
For this, the pup of Cadhan's brute
Now terrorized the Gleann's high route.

So Laeg   he rouses dazed Cú Chulainn
He points beyond the horse's skull and
There ahead the monster slabbers
Lickin round his canine stabbers
Drools for double helpin human flesh
Cú Chulainn's wounds now opened fresh
From all the chariot's buckin round
Arousin more the hungry hound
It leps and lands and sinks its fangs
Cú Chulainn's throat now feels the Pangs.

As if he didn't hurt enough
But as they say   when goin's tough
You know   he gets his Wild up very quick
His Torque   his Warp   his Battle Schtick
He gathers up what's left of him
And on his visage   girnin grim
Appears a look that's bloody mental
Bulgin eyes and buckin dental
Cú Chulainn bites the hound right back
Chows out its eyes till baest sees black.

And from the empty sockets sucks
The life blood from the Pesht and pucks
The shucked out carcass up Sliabh Gallon
So from that day   Bothar na Cuilleann
Was the name they gave that road
On which occurred this episode
When thirst mad hero werewolf turns
Spits greyhound blood before gut churns
    No dog flesh et   no ꝟeıs offend
Before he reaches journey's end.

II

And when they cross into Droim Ard
  Aromas grip their noses hard
A townland for *The Kaylie* famous
Where clanns of Liam and of Seamus
So close to strife but on the brink
Forget their rows and share a drink
Round Droim Ard druid Tataigh's fire
Where his Dair fare can damp the ire
Of billy butt and cuddy kick
Give big hot wounds a healin lick.

Tataigh's hearth is Hay barn warm
He welcomes all with equal charm
He sizes up Cú Chulainn's gore
And opens up his wee half door
*'Sit down ye boy ye take a pew
It luks like ye cud use a few
Meet Comhraic Sal and Donncha Sló
And hAraigh Got and Bolfionn Seo
Here in Droim Ard with yarn and air
They right the rift and tie the tear.'*

These local bards through aether lungs
Recite   delight   let loose their tongues
With rhymin tales of wile invention
One yarn called *Bone of Contention*
Recalls a time two boyos   dead
Come back to life as baests instead
One as ass and one as goat
Two divils at each other's throat
Like fools who fail to see faith war
As folly follied far too far.

Cú Chulainn   gulpin   drinks them in
Both poetry and poitín spin
Around his blattered head like stars
At first as salt in open scars
They pierce his every pore in pain
Half flaekin out   but in his brain

His inward eye he didn't know
He even had   begins to show
In flashes fast   the very scene
The bards spout out about the Screen.

It shows himself as in a glass
As first the goat and then the ass
Now billy buck   now cuddy mic
In mad shape shiftin flickers quick
Till ass from elbow he can't tell
For both are kilt and bent for hell
Naught left of them but one lone bone
Fanatic faith's contentious own
Cú Chulainn thinks he's bein" warned
A rhymin lesson partly larned.

There fifty drums of Dair he downed
Till in Droim Ard no more was found
But still Cú Chulainn needed more
To drench his gut and stanch his gore
And so begins the epic Crawl
From townland one to townlands all
All three and thirty[*] in Ꮑn Sᴄʀín
Where each produced a pure poitín
Each three and thirty times distilled
Religiously by druids skilled.

For in this mystic neck of woods
There dwelt a people ruled by druids
Who didn't care for sacrifice
But found that potions would suffice
To paecify the gods above
So harvestin the bounty of
The forest trees that there abound
Distillin essences they ground
That they might drink each universe
To alter worlds and times traverse.

Such spirits pure did not induce
Some drunken state of mind abuse
But might make drinkers wile impaired
And druids here were not prepared
To tolerate mad chariot drives
Riskin broken bones and lives
So Laeg he parks Cú Chulainn's car
Shank's marein it to high Cath Oir
Half draggin limp Cú Chulainn's frame
A mite revived but still sore lame.

---

   [*] There are actually 38 townands and at least 10 "sub-townlands" in Ballinascreen
but 33 was a mystical number in the ancient Celtic world.

◇

And on those lower Gallon braes
Cú Chulainn's spirits more would raise
When in a corner of that place
He found the dwellin full of grace
Of widow Cadhan   druidess
Who satisfied his thirstiness
With double fifty Cath Oir cups
Of finest Cath Oir Or he sups
Says he, as he was gettin full
'I'm on the mend, but still no bull.'

IIII

From there he drags his hefty butt
To Tonnach where he fills his gut
At druid Truaillean Dubh's abode
With Tonnach tOnnic by the load
He bokes his bulgin belly out
And bathes the townland in his gout
But not before he catches sight
A glimpse of space and time in flight
Of grand big dwellins there below
With many people runnin to and fro.

IIII

And having drunk the townland dry
He thinks he'll give Cloch Fionn a try
But this is Fionn McCumhaill's own turf
Where each who treads becomes his serf
So now the scene is surely set
For ructions Cloch Fionn won't forget
But when they meet at Brollaghan's
The druid serves ClochCollagins
Rich hazel nut extracted drinks
From bushes down Whitewater spinks.

That eases Fionn's protective mood
About his precious neighbourhood
That and brave Cú Chulainn's state
Whose wounds had almost sealed his fate
Make Fionn reluctantly decide
To be Cuchullain's local guide
For Fionn knows well the veils of Screen
That keep its verdant vales half seen
Knows all its covert ways and wiles
How its shape shiftin so beguiles.

Shape shifter that he is himself
Affords him passage like an elf
Through that tense surface liquid state
We see but cannot penetrate
Without drownin in its still well
That mirrors us as virtual
Fionn just sucks his thumb and drinks
Reflections shiftin as he thinks
He knows what bars the way within
Will melt as his cup's emptyin.

Cú Chulainn's much more in yer face
A warrior without a trace
Of doubt about what's hereabouts
He probes reality with clouts
His penetration's less with words
Than with slithers   spears and swords
And as for that ᵹᴀe boʟᵹᴀ gear
Well   that seems vergin on the queer
Though by all accounts his lovely wife
His Eimear   he loves more than life.

This force of nature meets his match
In Fionn's ability to watch
What's going on behind ᴀn Sᴄʀín
While Cú Chulainn takes life as seen
A bit of yang   a bit of ying
To have two halves is balancing
So when the spirits start to flow
It's arm in arm and on they'll go
It's three sheets to the wind all right
Blind leadin blind betimes sees light.

||||

As full as ticks they both soon are
Their enmity now mere meme war
Buck leppin up Stragh Mountain braes
While singin loud each other's praise
Till all An Scrín and Gleann Con Cadhain
Can hear their tuneless gulderin
Soon amplified with Straghtopup
Another class of High Coll Cup
That has them dancin wild sean nos
With stompin steps and song verbose.

⊥

This wild carouse just deepens druth
So off in search of Comhrac Uath
Which poitín punters long had known
Is often found near kin gravestone
Discreetly placed by druid Aodhaidh
Whose still dripped whitethorn juices dewy

In finest nectar bee sucked sips
Cú Chulainn gulps through broken lips
And feels it smoothe his harsh hacked tongue
Seep into every slash that stung.

A salve he shuns at first   then slaps
It into him   till Aodhaidh staps
This wile unseemly waste of taste
'Haen it   man dear   why all this haste?
Quet gulpin down this Comhrac Uath
It's not for druth   this font of youth.'
Cú Chulainn takes this counsel wise
Savourin sips of modest size
Its taste a revelation rare
Of Comhrac's haw pome scented air.

Cú Chulainn doesn't ponder deep
When he's not fightin he's asleep
But here he is on Comhrac braes
Seein things in different ways
Thanks to Aodhaidh's sage sip advice
He's noticin this gleann is nice
Whitewater river gurgles by
Birdsong bees   rabbit   butterfly
At peace   a while   he takes it in
Fionn watches with a knowin grin.

But Comhrac Uath   it can send
Untutored drinkers round time's bend
For soon Cú Chulainn starts to hear
A hellish grindin in his ear
Across the vale   a brutal blare
And damn the bit these heroes care
For Bolia's quarries crushin rock
The roar of which they've time unlocked
When monster carts haul gravel ore
The black pitch roads to Tobair Mór.

卌

This look forward grieves their minds
As does the view so far behind
When next they visit Ballybriest
To find ancestral ones deceased
Their mothers' fathers' giants' grave
Their fathers' mothers' death enclave
They head for Ned the Seanachie's
A tall tale Brollaghan and he's
The very man can give them cheer
Raise the spirits on the bier.

And many were the lies that night
Of spirits seen and second sight
Of time long gone and down the line
All fuelled by a Ruiswine
Ned's druid brother had distilled
From rush and elderberry milled
As turf fire flame made shadows flit
To mingle with the shades that lit
And lingered for a bit of crack
Before they faded back to black.

T

Back down to Breacach through black night
Across Blackwater's foggy light
They ceilidh in the house of Greith
Who brews a brilliant Breacach Beith

So many dripers drained the pair
They floated through the misty air
Made up of spirits more than rain
So time and space shift yet again
To tell a vision aerial
And weave a yarn aethereal.

A story of an age to come
When uisce bheatha demon rum
Would be condemned as somethin vile
And that for a good long while
Kings in charge outlawed the crathur
Allowing only stuff called aether
So up in those wild Sperrin hills
Like Breacach with its many stills
These little aether dens cropped up
Where druid vessels got topped up.

But back in time with boul Cú Chulainn
He and Fionn seek out The Uillean
A famed delicious Díseart treat
A honeysuckle melon sweet
So succulent it turns mens' heads
While stupefied upon their beds
To Sidhe siren songs they hear
Bemusing softly in their ear.
'Beware' says Fionn 'of Díseart charms
Its drink your sense of real disarms.'

'A troll and tip they traipse this place
Buttin holes in time and space
For hidden in the shugh and ditch
Are forces dark that bate and snitch
And planted in the forests green

Especially on each branch unseen
Are eyes and ears that assay us
That given time will   aye   array us
As billys rise from duchull pile
To dunt the rising sons of Niall.'

'Down in the maze of paths and trails
The underworld of Díseart wails
Whitewater sounds that should bring peace
Become a noise that will not cease
Its whispers turned to banshee screams
Till Shibbigh spirits stalk your dreams
When hunger strikes your jaws agape
The gates of Hell block your escape
And when your time down there is up
The silent ghosts still with you sup.'

2. Sé Bhaile Taes

T
The mornin revenants dispersed
The heroes wish to be immersed
Upon arisin from their beds
To bathe and aese their aechin heads
And findin waters Black and White
Too shallow for their girth and might
Climb the hills to An Abhainn Riabhach
Where there's a kettle on the way
'Fulacht Fiadh of the gods'   says Fionn
'Manannan's Fled Goibhniu Skin.'

Cú Chulainn   wrecked from climbin hard
Could hardly spaek   so high this ard
But lossin tongue was just begun
When he caught sight in shaft of sun
Of lovely liquid lough on tap
That glittered at each wavy lap
To Cú Chulainn's druth severe
It seemed a bright brim winkin beer
If Screen was one big flagon jug
Then this the mouth of that big mug.

Cú Chulainn throws off all his gear
And plunges in the boggy beer
The bog brown Bolia boulfull sink
Where cloudy gods drop in to drink
Deep dippin down their misty tongues
Lappin lough   fillin liquid lungs

There's not a lot to go around
But cloudy gods have never found
A more upliftin mountain dew
Than this wee lough's bogwater brew.

Cloudgods up here put on a show
For this wee mirror which they know
Will kiss them with its rushy stout
And rush them dark and full to spout
On every townland in the Screen
One final lap of lough poitín
One kiss to gorge the great cloudgods
One last tae drap so hefted Clods
Can lash down on Moyola's plain
Pishin   boggin   bucketin rain.

Cú Chulainn floatin lookin up
Seein the gods begin to sup
'Sláinte Scamall'   he roars on high
Then goes down to swallow the sky
Swallows swoop the surface skim
Scoopin midges away from him
He lets the cloud reflections seep
Into his scars   sword sores so deep
Scamall sláinte makes him hael
What aels him aesed by their pale ael.

III

But now it's time for soulful soak
From this townland whose druid folk
Distil and spill a Wee Black Tinne
A golden tae of holly gin
And spike it with a seamróg shaec
To stanch all wounds   spear   sword or snake.
Though this will make the slap a gunk
And tip the tipplers triple drunk
Imaginin divinity   in duplicate or trinity.

Whereas in truth they've been well oiled
Duped   tripped up   tricked   trefoiled.
And presently they'll see the past
And future as a dream forecast
In which the bards who love this place
Consider it a hallowed space
To gather words and ancient bones
And blend them in their rhymin tones
To conjure   in their turn   a phrase
In which a holy man they'll raise.

No druid him   this shepherd saint
Their ancient rites his main complaint
And bein' there on wee lough shore
To prove his spells superior
He calls a cant across the lake
That bids Cú Chulainn to awake
And sure enough he does arise
Not from the hell the saint implies
But from bog water where he lies
Buck naked   sunk up to his eyes.

The saint has pulled this one before
To make Cú Chulainn live once more
He thinks he's got the trick down pat
Convincin kings with stunts like that
But this he fails to realize
These druid boys to him are wise
Such feats of raisin from the dead
Are planted in his holy head
When he sups druid Seoirse's best
The Wee Black Tinne for honoured guest.

The trinity of time on show
Throws the three in future flow
The bog aquaekin with the sound
Of Breachach rocks now crushed and ground
The limpid lake a rippled glass
That mirrors not just clouds that pass
But towerin trefoil twurlin blades
That slice the air like big turf spades
Three sheets to the wind revolve
The burnin up the earth to solve.

The saint gets on his *Hi Hi* horse
Enraged at such a future course
He crams his crook up oxter tight
And runs and tilts with all his might
Chargin windy seamróg towers
Callin down all heaven's powers
To turf them down and burlin cease
Returnin Abhainn Riabach's rushy peace
But all in vane his charge is stumped
Thrice he's thumped and in lough dumped.

Our heroes fish him with his crook
His pishyprick life-saving hook
And reel him through the rushy shore
Half-drownded   nearly-thirded sore
Fractious effin blindin still intact
Them laughin at his quick soak act
A wee smile breaks the grim phisog
'Aye, thank ye for the rush through bog
To bring this fish up from the deep
Now on this tummock   let me sleep.'

He dreams that he is satisfied
Not just Cú Chulainn has defied
The laws of grim fatality
But Fionn's now too reality
This miracle a two for one
His mission here is surely done
So partin ways our heroes head
For An Tullaigh Bhric where they are fed
And watered by Mac Giolla Bridhe
Scholastic druid   true and tried.

From forest trees up Dabhagh way
His elder aether potent tae
So volatile this Ruis drink
It rushes them to outer brink
Of worlds so clearly not their own
Damnear into wild Tír Eoghain
And in the bogs of Tullaigh Bhric
From all these potions take their pick
Thus channelled back to childhood years
Setanta's hurlin with his peers.

So Fionn   fifteen joins in to play the game
Agin Setanta's team takes aim
And soon they're scattered all around
Every teammate hits the ground
Till only these two boyos stand
Now one-on-one and hand-to-hand
They range across Sé Bhaile wide
To score and tackle and collide
Setanta guards the Broughderg end
Fionn does   of course   Fionnglen defend.

To mark the march of their endzones
Each posts a pair of standing stones
Glenviggan rocks Setanta's line
Cavanreagh boulders Fionn's define
ᴘᴏᴄ ꜰᴀᴅᴀ here's four townlands long
At this Setanta's caman's strong
He's got McCumhaill on the run
Despite defence of trip and stun
He fires points o'er hills and knolls
Beyond Cnoc Mór and into Goles.

Again the Screen's rocked to its core
With all the din and wild uproar
Of slither splintered poc cracked heads
Till both of them in shattered shreds
Collapse at half time in Moyard
To take refreshment from the bard
Whose wee black tinne has been refilled
With honeysuckle draughts distilled
But this time time goes in reverse
Fast forward future past inverse.

The latter half of this wild match
They boot a bladder   ban the catch
Fionn's skill at this is to the fore
His kicks oft endin in a score
He's managed well by druid guile
Another Brollaghan with style
Of that ancient Celtic order
Who don't care about the border
Between Uladh and the other
Part still causin all the bother.

This oul druid gets excited
When he leads his men united
To a win or daecent score
Agin the likes of Tobair Mór
So here he is now guidin Fionn
A southerner who is no kin
And Cú Chulainn he gets rattled
Thinks of southerners he's battled
Keeping Uladh safe from Connacht
And her cattle raids upon it.

Setanta's lossin now to Fionn
He's lettin far too many in
Fionn is runnin rings around him
As his dribble moves astound him
And Fionn harps on about his skill
Makin' Setanta fit to kill
So what to do? He nicks the posts
To shut up Fionn's swelled-headed boasts
And sets a precedent for years
Sé Bhaile goalposts disappears.

He gathers up each standin stone
And flings them into far Tír Eoghain
Where one that lands in Achadh Uí Aráin
There fallin near   so goes the yarn
The head of one who'd often been
Hearing callins from An Scrín
Where he'd find his new vocation
Strict devotion - faith and nation
And many sins of Scrín he'd blame
On druids   drink and foreign game.

26

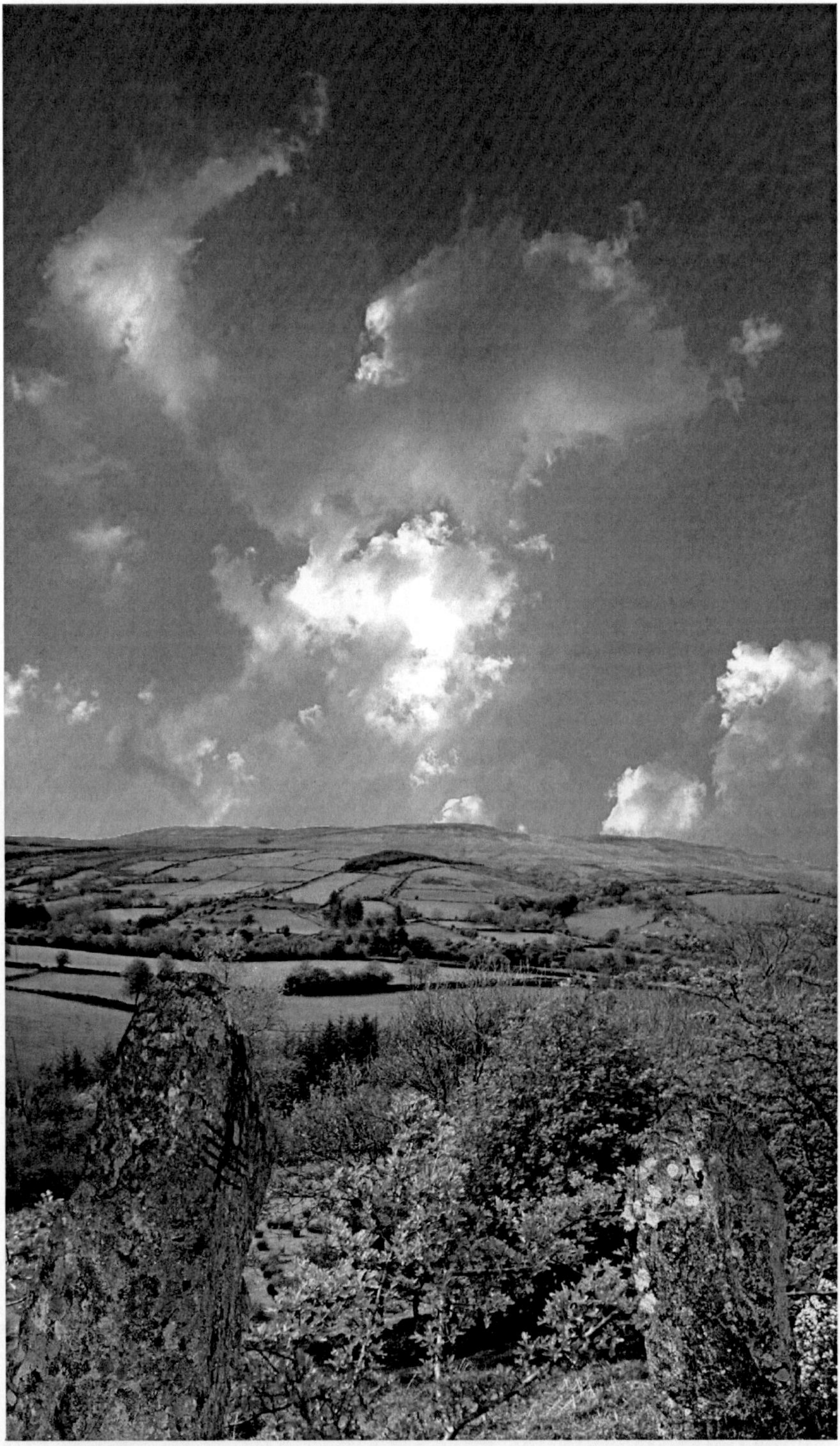

Nor will cleric disapproval stop
In Móin na Chongna where they drop
Blootered from pursuit athletic
In need of fluid anaesthetic
Cú Chulainn's wounds now newly aechin
From hard fought games just undertaken
But this place sports a healin wine
From Móin na Chongna Muin vine
That grows along Moyola's stream
Where fishers teem and lovers dream.

The two boys lap a lep in time
To find themselves in sleep sublime
On a hill above that silver stream
Deep within that star struck dream
That has them lie in contemplation
Gazin' up at constellation
Cú Chulainn   when suddenly they hear
A bell belt out increasin clear
Above them, they soon realize
Is fallin fast from starlit skies.

'Look there'   says Fionn   'below yer belt
Some sort of bell is being knellt
It's set alight and headin here
Them shootin stars I've seen   no fear
But shootin bells is mighty queer
And this one's ringin loud and clear
I think we better up and gone
It might jist neb you   landin on
You   maybe all them Muin jars
Have us seein more than stars.'

Before the bell could take its toll
They pull a sprightly spring and roll
The bell rim cuts a ring so deep
It would have sliced them in their sleep
'Hells bells' says Fionn 'That's very close
The gods are gettin bellicose.'
Just then   out from behind some whuns
Another of the saintly ones
Calls out 'Get away to hell
Or I'll be ringin your death knell.'

'And who are you' Cú Chulainn asks,
'To take us so roughly to task?'
'None of your oul heathen guff' says he
'All you need know is I'm holy   see
And here to rid this place of you
Druid ridden pagans who screw
And drink and have too many gods
So out of here you drunken sods
I'm building here a holy place
Where thon bell fell from heaven space.'

'I tried to build two times before
But some Pesht or other knocked them o'er
I'll bet you two eejits tummeled
Them when yous run mad and stummled
Round these hills playing foreign games
Sure you heathens make a haems
Of everything   behine me Satan!
Or by god I'll have yous baeten
God's curse upon the pair of ye
Yer big but I'm not scared of ye.'

This wild coorse sermon and tirade
On Cú Chulainn an impression made
Though in a mellow mood   his Warp
Began to build and bristle sharp
He raised his fist as if to strike
But Fionn   as always   statesmanlike
Stepped in and drew the warrior aside
Thus preventin homicide
'Go aesey friend   be calm be still
You cannot What Ye Call Him kill.'

28

Cú Chulainn gnashed his teeth and turned
Despite the way his ire burned
'This churlish churchman needs to watch
His mouth and back or he will catch
A hammerin but since he's brave
Enough to stand up to us and rave
I'll spare him and will even aid
Him till his foundation's laid.'
'It must be Móin na Chongna wine'
Thinks Fionn   'that's made him so benign.'

And sure enough Cú Chulainn goes
Off to Beagh Mór and throws
Back a wild clatter of rocks
To be foundation buildin blocks
Near martyrin in their flight
The holy tarra anchorite
But three unite to work as one
And in no time at all it's done
The monk surprised has to admit
'I've built a shrine owes some brave bit ...

◇

... to these two hallion heathen men
So he begins to see them then
As not so bad   'I've been too hard
On them   I'll traet them in Maigh Ard'
And in a place where sheepmen rest
They call in for a feed of best
Maigh Ard Oir that lubricates
The joints of these three builders mates
Till loosened up all three begin
To dance with girls who've found they're in.

Although he thinks such dances foreign
To his code that keeps his sporran
Firmly in its place   the well oiled monk
Begins to reel with all he's drunk
And singin too to every girl
Who'd do a jig with him and whirl
So now this place's reputation's set
Where drink and women you can get
A place for none or any god
Where communion's meanin's broad.

The three boys dance a holy show
To music that is all the go
Played by Gleann Seáin folk who know
How curly tunes slide off the bow
To jewelled twang from old banseo
To mickle whistle notes that blow
To singin strings of chords that flow
Like streams that frankly morph and grow
Into broad Moyola or the Roe
With sprickly backs and trout in tow.

So taken by this harmony
Cú Chulainn and the monk agree
To defer all hostilities
So close are their identities
The mornin after time turns round
The monk is nowhere to be found
Cú Chulainn feels a presence passed
Inside of him an icon cast
The monk and warrior combined
Their stories forever intertwined.

☩

With last night's music in their heads
The pair along Moyola treads
To An Leaba where they drink Onn wine
And hear its stories that define
The character and soul of Scrín
From then to now and in between
The wines are from a whinney bush
That grow among the ditches lush
The tales are from a seanachie
Whose home they meet in genially.

Those who call the whin bush useless
Except in spring to golden ditches
Haven't sipped its honeyed juices
Distilled to bring out all its riches
Fine wine within whin botany.
If sip they do they slip through time's
Ever onward monotony
And skip time keepin and its chimes
So back and forth they go with aese
As far and often as they plaese.

In time the seanachie will warn
Our two time travellers he met
'It's about time you have to larn
The deeper down in time you get
The more times people think you're mad
Like take the time this man and I'd
Undertaken in spare time we had
To take times when and who had died
From tombstones time had beaten down
Till in time near underground.'

'There we were in Stragh graveyard
Upstanding men of dignity
He a bier and body guard
Me a scribe and seanachie
Crawling on our hands and knees
Sometimes laid out upon our backs
And passersby who witnessed these
Two stretched on sacred ground made cracks
'Have yous spirits in yous or what?
Lyin with the dead like that.'

29

This grave warnin duly heeded
Our heroes bid the seanachie so long
And through an Leaba rinth proceeded
Still amazed by whun wine strong
They cross a ford to Domhnall Lea
To find a home long settled there
Belongin to a family
Of hardy upright folk who care
About faith community and land
With strength of spirit　will and hand.

The peace of this idyllic lea
Is broken only by a muffled beat
Comin from a shade's vicinity
Which Fionn inspects with care discreet
Before openin a padded pod
Rigged up to quell the blast within
Which damn near rips apart his bod
Such is the force of rhythmic din
That rolls out now and rocks his ears
And nearly busts their drums he fears.

Cú Chulainn soon comes on the run
To save his guide from harm's way
Thinkin a battle has begun
With all this wild cacophony
But very soon they both begin
To shake their hips and hop their feet
To rave and rap and try to sing
So infectious is the beat
That this young buck inside the pod
Rigs up and gigs there on his tod.

When stopped he tells them when and where
They'll find a feast of similar sound
Of fado rhythms blastin air
If someday they're Maigh dTamlacht bound
'We'll head for Eagle's Rock'　they say
*'When we get over being deef
To Gleann Gomhna now we're on our way
That quiet gleann will bring relief.'*
They little know what lies in store
As they dander towards Cnoc Mór.

3. Cnoc Mór Craes

||||

Before they reach the Gomhna glen
Fionn turns and grips his drinkin friend
'What happens here'   says he   'stays here
This townland's poitín has no peer
But first you must its custom keep
You cannot drink it clad in sheep
Or any fleece but in the raw
This is the Glen of Strippers' law
That only those without their clothes
Will taste the way the heather grows.'

Before Cú Chulainn has the time
To show off all his manly prime
He sees a sight upon a Green
Unique to this remotest Screen
A paradise of strippers rude
Buck leppin as they laugh in lewd
Song   loudly joyous in their cups
And in their midst a druid sups
'Clan Mac Na Midhe'   says Fionn   'brews here
Your purest Úr to strip your rear.'

Our kiltless duo now advance
Onto The Green where heifers dance
Cú Chulainn's eyes now lukin here
Now there   bravely tryin not to leer

Laughter rings out through the glen
At his war-wounded pouch and pen
But when he's had a draught of Úr
He doesn't care a damn how poor
His parted parts to peers appear
And so joins in without a fear.

'Up here'   says Fionn   'on Cnoc Mór braes
Where strippin down is all the craes
The druids know the ancient tongues
In touch with teeth and throat and lungs
The words ancestral close to source
Of mountain air's full rough gael force
That scribes its marks on stone and wood
Conveyin nature's message crude
Glen Gomhna is god Oghma's home
Where native tongue is free to roam.

Cloud spirit Úr sits on Cnoc Mór
Him thrustin up to meet her mist
The icy blast his round head bore
Unleashin heaven's lashin kist
The thunder tongue of mountain din
Licks down his slopes through lush loose lips
Cú Chulainn feels his war geld pair
Begin to heal as in he slips
His pouch brim full with Úr to spare
His pen again sword mended quare.

'Go deep   peel back'   says Fionn   'pare in
Push back to thon first words intone
Glen Gomhna's Oghma origin
This mount is Oghma's standing stone
A bulgin bolga broad domain
And here on this sun facin' slant
The tongue's first taste for words regain
The grunt and groan   the puff and pant
Whistle whine hiss roar blow blast and rant.'

As up they go to bonny Dún
The hear an air drift with the breeze
A barely perceptible tune
That whispers in the rustlin trees
To draw the travellers towards a brae
Where a Ceallach druid's at a still
That's bubblin and whistlin away
'Sit down'   says he   'and drink your fill
This Dún Sail stuff will do you good
Elixir from the sally wood.'

ᚌ

No sooner had they raised a Sail
Than the tune they'd faintly heard before
Is heightened to a major scale
By an ancient harpin troubadour
Playin on a dragon headed harp
His eyes a vacant blindman's stare
His clawlike nails so lightnin sharp
The notes pour out and fill the air
A symphony of shinin strings
Sails down the wind and round Dún rings.

A Ceallach harpwright stands nearby
Intent on every clear plucked note
That from the harper's fingers fly
'Good'   the blind one says   'and what you wrote
On it is perfect   'Queen of Musick   aeh?
A royal instrument indeed
The Bonny Prince will hear this play
And know this sound none will exceed
Tell me   Cormac   the wood you use
That can so well seduce the Muse."

'Bog sally'   says the old harpwright
'Dug from the moss not far from Craobh
Well aged since Noah's time   it might
Even have been round when Eve
Seduced yer man to play her tune.'
All this crack about seductions
Gets our heroes hormones hoppin
But now the chance of wilder ructions
Suddenly there is no stoppin
When in their midst appears a lass
That no young buck with eyes could pass.

The harper smiles   plays on like hell
The harpwright frowns for this cailín
Is his only daughter Nell
The apple of the eye of Screen
That every local bard and lad
Has mused about and mooned about
Till they've been driven nearly mad
With lustin and with love devout
Here dancin to the harper's tune
While these two strangers stand and swoon.

She moves with an unearthly grace
Her feet so lightly touchin ground
Her slender curves reshape the space
That's ornamented with the sound
Of harp and whisper of her breath
Cú Chulainn's smitten as is Fionn
They'd fight right now unto the death
If given half a chance to win
This beauty who has cast a spell
That's turned their heads and hearts to swell.

She dances in between the pair
Givin each the faintest whiff
Of fragrant breath and silky hair
That builds in them resolve so stiff
And Fionn is moved to tend to her
To take her hand and join the dance
But Cú Chulainn won't surrender her
So in a threesome takes his chance
Tangled in that oul triangle
That jingle jangle wile fandangle.

They're cookin like a still in Craobh
That's doin' more than bubble now
The kettle has begun to heave
The worm is kickin up a row
The peaceful townland feels the heat
The risin tension throbs and prods
Each force that wont accept defeat
Or see the good in others' gods
A potent blend of lust and soil
Brings manly passions to the boil.

Inevitably there's a slip
With both in passion's thrall and thirst
A spin   a swing   a dunt   a trip
The oul primeval big bang burst
The still and stillness blow their stacks
The knight of Fianna unloads
The Uladh warrior attacks
The spirit of the time explodes
And all of Craobh and Dún are lit
As if by lightnin they've been hit.

Blasted fragments of the still
Are scattered wide like sown seeds
The harper   harpwright   dancers spill
Like timeblown dandelion weeds
And when the cosmic dust cloud settles
The two antagonists of late
Find themselves in stingin nettles
Again defrocked they lie prostrate
Before a Beannchrann Bealtaine pyre
Burnt out   in need of drink to cool their fire.

###

Their arses hot   their ardour cooled
They run for cover in the Glibe
Not wantin to be ridiculed
By three lovely lassies from Beannchrann tribe
Who chase them till they're near Dunsinn
A druid haven where they learn
The Glibe's own grog   its Gedal gin
Is made from Beannchrann bracken fern
Fiddleheadin all who drink it in
Our heroes reconciled again.

Transported now by Beannchrann tope
They spiral round time's endless line
And find they've spun a massive rope
So tough and taut this twisted twine
Its tension must be infinite
A battle ranges for its length
Two teams of Titans haul it tight
With gulders to increase their strength
For here in Beannchrann's rollin hills
Live men who pull with iron wills.

Cú Chulainn can't resist a war
Tuggin at his heart strings   war's his life
His challenge issued with a roar
He'll take on all at this rope strife
But one steps forward from the crowd
One Huge Hero known hereabouts
Judgin by the cheers that ring aloud
And this boy's answer leaves no doubts
'I'll take you on ye boy ye   aye
And baet ye aesey in a tie.'

Huge arms and hands adorn this man
And soon Cú Chulainn finds it rough
To keep his grip or take a stand
Agin this Beannchrann Champion tough
Three days and nights they pull and yank
Each other half way round An Scrín
From Comhraic hills to Spelhoagh turf bank
And all the townlands in between
Till finally the rope it snaps
And the two contestants collapse.

'Not bad'   the boul Cú Chulainn cries
'For a local gype you've got balls.'
'Not bad yearself'   the boy replies
'For a stunted gulpin who calls
Himself a warrior knight'
This Beannchrann banter back and forth
Till insults nearly end in fight
But both have given all they're worth
So knackered they just flake amach
And retire to a ceilí teach.

The owner of this ceilí teach
A member of the Clann Ceallach
Serves up a potent Beannchrann tae
That sends both foes and Fionn astray
Into that twilight zone of time
Disruptin reason's rule and rhyme
So seanachies and bards appear
From every era front and rear
To spout and sing the praises loud
Of families of the Ceallach crowd.

Every Ceallach at this ceili
Was hAmídh   Phidir or a Neilí
Or Domhnall Michil Madam dames
Or Dens and Chuits or other names
Like Micí Eoghain   Micí Pól
Or Mhicí   Pít or Seanín Pól
Or a Tríona or from the ranks
Of Bhachadhs   Damnics or the Francs
From all around the Clann Ceallach
Gather here to shoot the crack.

34

From Beannchrann Dún Craobh Stragh and Leacht
In this renovated ceilı ceach
Not long ago a rundown shack
But now a place for lookin back
For reminiscin   keepin track
Of yarns that aegin memories lack
For seanachies and bards who rack
Their ancient brains amnesiac
To find ısceach the horde   the stack
Of stories   poems   songs and crack.

The Ceallach ceili goes all night
And luckily without a fight
For some of them are crabbit folks
Who often give but can't take jokes
When songs and poems lyrical
Do take the mic satirical
The oul ancestral memories
Begin to haunt and hemorrhage
There will be blood and that in piles
When some young buck and oul boy riles.

But on this night the turf fire glows
As Beannchrann Tae in torrents flows
And all the Ceallachs get along
Through lively crack and funny song
Cú Chulainn marvels at the scene
The harmony he finds in Screen
Until one bard begins to spout
'The Ballad of Cú Chulainn's Rout'
Is it prophesy or history?
For Cú Chulainn it's a mystery.

The bard who rhymes Cú Chulainn's fall
The burns of Dún's own Seánín Pól
Now daels our warrior a shock
Cú Chulainn doesn't place much stock
In passin or in closin time
Or baetin time to tellin rhyme
Yet here he is in this bard's mind
In a time before or time behind
And in a place he might have been
Another townland of The Screen.

Says Seánín Pól   'I heard these rhymes
From Droim Dearg's own sharp Diamin mind
A bard in tune with ancient times
Who spoke like this to warn our kind.'
...
'I mine them well   them days of old
When them Phoenicians came to Screen
And offered for our Dair   their gold
But we said   naw   we're no sidhe been
Where men get rich beyond their due
From Cnoc Mór mountain commons brew.'

'Our Cnoc Mór Dair was traded fair
No merchant men to profit from
What acorn gives without a tare
Its tannin twang of oaken drum
But now fool's gold   Phoenician coin
Was turnin heads from common health
If only druids here would join
In makin' Dair a source of wealth
To all this gold round Cnoc Mór hill
Comes Duna Dirigean Mercmobille.'

II

'A greedy armoured foreign queen
Who tholed no check to her broad path
A hard case gulpin gorb gombeen
Rough shod ridin'   cuttin a swath
Her belch alone enough to kill
Her beamer eyes her fartin roar
Her fierce fourlegged spinnin skill
That crushes hounds   brock   bird and boar
Who   but that great Hound of Ulster
Could take on this raevin rabid monster?'

'The call goes out for boul Cú Chulainn
To save us from the Mercmobille
So racin' north The Hound full willin
To tackle such a brutal ill
But first to stiffen oaken strength
He visits druid Maolagain
Where sittin suppin Dair at length
He hears oul news of her again
Of druids Mercmobille attacked
Rudhraic   Mac Uirc and Mac Cormac.

'She's killin us'   says Mac Cormac
'She Beetles round each loanin track
Especially when she's drunk n mad
Her crushin weight and race is bad
But what is worse IT takes her over
Some kind of Hound   aye   Land Rover
This Hounda hell can Ford the burns
A Foe cuss hard that makes bad turns
Crosser than a curse   no Mercy class
And forbye   forces Pass at pass.'

'Cú Chulainn thinks this Foe cuss might
Be his worst enemy in fight
Is she Angle Goth or Franc?' says he
'Some folks waggin   say she be
A Gee Em up or Em Gee too
She Leks us to be in her view
With her behind her visor dark
Shapeshiftin gear with us her mark
Far worse than Medb the Connacht queen
She scars the pleasant lanes of Screen.'

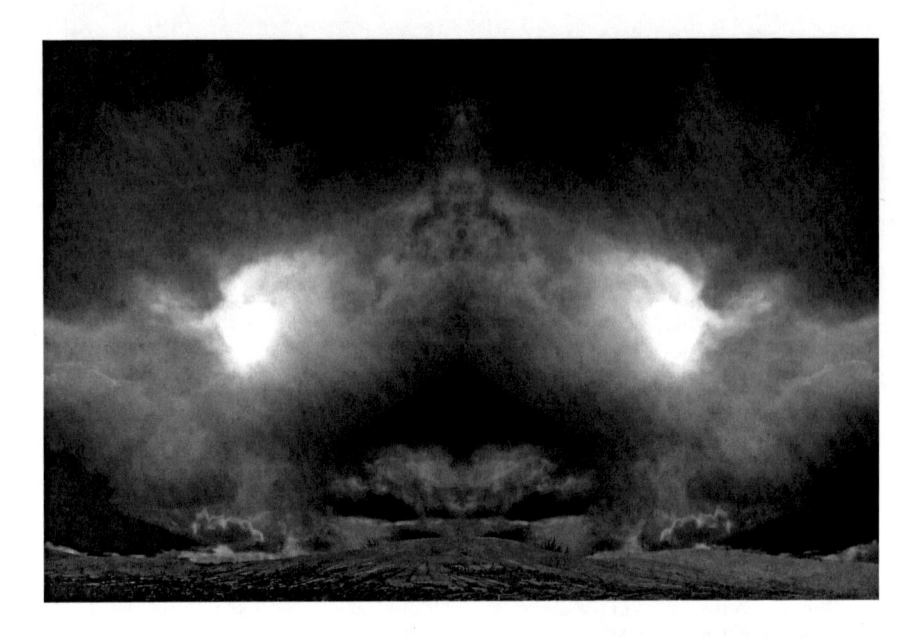

'She coorts us in with Regent charms
Her hard sleek Shell her slick inside
Her Husky purr her huggin arms
But very soon she's just another ride
Her feistithe grindin clutchin grasp
She's so tarra queen Imperial
She burns the air and makes men gasp
Becomes a skull king scavengin
A Total ragin Morrigan.'

'She gorribs bones skin guts and brains
Of kin interred long centuries
Our deep ancestors' last remains
Beneath the soils and sands and seas
Now drilled   sucked   dug and desecrate
Her bothar smoothed by corpse pitch paved
To slake her self accelerate
Her time is coin and must be saved
Burnin past   roastin future kin
Unbridled lust for speed in her thick skin.'

'She drills her claws in deep and wide
And sucks black scum that oozes up
For every jag of speed she ride
Her druth in need of endless sup
And from her astra be pee trails
Sprayin scent   rippin sod and turf
Spawnin countless cunty Cluain twins
That swally whole each smitten serf
Who used to walk the ways of Screen
And give the time of day to all they seen'

'She sounds like wan right wile cute hoor'
Says Cú Chulainn   lookin pale
'I think my chances awful poor
But I'll sniff out her drunken trail
She sounds like yer man Grendel's ma
Mere woman   maneater craeter
Wance insider   meet kelpie da
She's jist bait for pater waiter
The drownin capall ola stallion
The buckin bronco drink in hallion.'

'He's the wan yer after not the ma
He's the slippy bogger drags ye in
Ola Mór Dubh Mercmobille   the da
Heady horse power swerve and spin
Wan buckin hoof on this slick steed
Yer saddled hooked and in his grip
Feelin free and timeless   gainin speed
He ducks ye deep for yer last dip
You can't let Ola Mór give you the slip.`

'His slick black hard heart pumpin fire
His dragon breath   a rank reek foul
His spurtin veins turn earth to mire
The ϡeıs to come on new and oul
He doesn't count his hollow cost
It's hidden in his gombeen drive
To conquer all till all is lost
A show aghast   none left alive'
Cú Chulainn glimpses future fast
Famine strife and desert blast.

Cú Chulainn fortified goes out
To sit all night and wait the rout
Where now Droim Dearg townland lies
When late he sees her blindin eyes
Come blazin through the Dubhgall ford
Then roar like some loud hummer horde
Careerin down upon his seat
That makes him rise take to his feet
And charge the baest at her right flank
To tear at her front spinnin shank.

Cú Chulainn's belted by the baest
Duna deterred not in the laest
Duntin Cú Chulainn on his head
Whaeld by her hard bloated tread
'I'll get ye the next time ye brute'
Cries Cú Chulainn limpin in pursuit
'This is a Hound aye Hounda Hell
Me head is ringin me own death knell
This Hound is heavy hard and haest
No camán poc can geg this baest.'

Exhausted tired overrun
'That was wan wile wicked crack
I took' says he 'a far worse stun
Than any Queen Medb bull attack
I'm goin' to have to use the head
This is no hound or bull I know
This brute runs over ye yer dead
Now let me think what kind of blow
Could I dael to this foe female
To rid the Screen of her wassael?'

'A cunning plan like one thought out
By Fionn McCumhaill who thinks outside
His skin to what's around about
Like thon big standing stone beside
The burn to Dubhgall river ford
I've got it now it's her Cú Chulainn's heel
Who lives by sword will die by sword
If stoned she wants then stoned she'll feel
So into Maolagain for a dram
Then off to the burn for the Ogham Slam.'

In spite of feelin bothar kill
He ropes the mighty Ogham stone
And scores on it the name Mobille
And drags it heaving   moan by groan
Fornenst the ford on far burn side
Then waits for Duna's fartin roar
As she comes back from her Cross ride
Before she fords the ford once more
Cú Chulainn's camán whacks a poc
That cracks her visor like a rock.

Distracted by the crack attack
She does not see the standing stone
But caroms of its hefty back
And through the air in flames is thrown
The sparks of armour scrapin rock
Ignitin gutfull aether spray
In one tremendous red hot shock
That lights the sky as far away
As Carnanelly and Cilcar
Carnamoney   Carndonagh and Catar.

Cú Chulainn won that battle great
But not the war on Mercmobille
For down by Cluain for five mile straight
You'll see her brood the bothar fill
Or through Cnoc Dubh to Tobair Mór
The snaekin trail of her dark ranks
Or round the Cross the constant roar
Of Mobille hordes round buried tanks
Down guzzlin gullets gallons pour
The slimy spawn of Ola Mór.'

Cú Chulainn is amazed at this
For as he listened to the bard
He felt himself and Fionn amiss
Half there   half not and off his guard
But when the rhymer reached his end
From Droim Dearg to the Dubhgall ford
They see themselves again descend
Across to Móin na Nionadh toward
A stand of oak trees on a hill
Where there's a druid standin still.

This is the druid son of Mídhe
The bard who served the Clan of Niall
Who did not pay the promised fee
For services poetical
And so the Midhes they turned to trade
In meat and drink instead of rhyme
And one of them   young Loughlin   made
His name in Screen about this time
When drunken daelers showed dissent
In Móin na Nionadh in his tent.

One rowdy cattle daeler yells
'A tent's no place to take a glass
We'd lek some comfort for oursels'
Not one to let a good dael pass
Loughlin ups and builds a place
But in Maigh Chaolain where the Fair
Would be a cattle daelin base
And many sons of Midhe reigned there
One long dynasty of druids
Daelin in the spirit fluids.

But back now to Cú Chulainn's time
(If time there is or time there was)
At the oaken stand where wine sublime
Makes him in Móin na Nionadh pause
To stop and stand with Fionn again
And look upon The Screen anew
Its Sperrin vistas now and then
Its evershiftin playful view
And see himself   Setanta   play
Sent out alive on time delay.

✝ ⅠⅠⅠⅠ

The druid cooks a splendid fix
From Nion ash and Muin vine
To make the Móin na Nionadh mix
That he'll distil and then refine
And give his guests now just arrived
Battle weary from Droim Dearg
And from this drink a dunt derived
A jolt of energetic erg
To fire up their flaggin spirits
Make them once again time's tourists.

The druid's shape will change at will
From son of Mídhe to son of Bheath
To son of Seain from son of Dubhghaill
To Mac anFhailghigh to this day

And he had a tale   a vision
Of spirit wide across The Screen
Inspired by a hero who'd arisen
In a way not previously seen
Who from this place had grown
From Móin na Nionadh's very own.

When Cú Chulainn hears the name
That this local hero's Coileain
That his prowess and his fame
Matches that of boul Cú Chulainn
He nearly has a spasm fightin fit
'Is he my cousin? What's his game?
I'll challenge him and bravely pit
Me strength and skill against his claim
To bein' champion   of what?
Pigskin catch and kick combat?'

They call this Coileain from his rest
(Sometimes he helped the druid still)
And hooped in red across his breast
He makes his entrance on the hill
A man of Sperrin mettle tall
Defender of The Screen and more
In his left hand a pigskin ball
And in his right The Grail he bore
*"I'll meet ye on the field of Straw
Prepare to lose or at most draw!"*

"I've baeten kingdoms in me day
Dumped the Dubhs in their black pool
Sent Tír Eoghain on its way
And as for you or Fionn MacCumhaill
Ard Macha and Cill Dara boys
I'll boot yous up to Craig na Shoke!"
Cú Chulainn doesn't lose his poise
'On those words I'll make you choke'
Fionn to danger's never deaf
So wisely he decides to ref

Such motor skills the three possessed
They fly through Dún and Díseart quick
But reachin Straw and looking west
The sun has set where they would kick
Cú Chulainn says "What good is this?
It's dark! We'll never see the ball!"
'Just wait'   says Fionn "There'll be a switch."
And in a flash the gloomy pall
Is bathed in brightest northern lights
"Magic"   Cú Chulainn says in awe
It's lek a trick of light in Straw!"

So in the Celtic twilight glow
These heroes clash in deadly match
Kickin   punchin   hand to toe
And half the country comes to watch
Every woman   man   and waen
Who should have long been fast asleep
Come flowin up Séan Mullagh lane
And Clogh Fionn way to braes so steep
They all can see each thump that's struck
Each slip and slither in Straw muck.

For on this night the heavens open
A deluge rarely seen before
Moyola's banks were far from copin'
As every shugh and burn would pour
Across the land and flood each stragh
So now this contest would proceed
In pools of water   muck and glar
But no one there paid any heed
Though all were drinched right to the bone
Sunk deep within the twilight zone.

The heroes claw through thickest clabber
The pigskin heavy   slippy   greased
When deep below this field of slabber
The dam that was is now released
And from the slime of ancient lint
A slick maneater surfaces
Cú Chulainn's stuck and cannot sprint
His jaws agape at what's aris
The slimy brute dives down his throat
And in his gut begins to bloat.

His guts half eaten by this devil
He dammed and gutted starts to howl
The playing field no longer level
Fionn whistles loudly for a foul
The free kick given seems unfair
Awarded to this Coileain boy
But Fionn is crafty and aware
He sucks his thumb and plots his ploy
He knows his way around this game
He'll save Cú Chulainn just the same.

Despite the frogspawn bog he's in
The Móin na nIonadh boy lets fly
And hoofs like hell the slick pigskin
Cú Chulainn dodgin it   leps high
And turns his back to save his bag
To taste his own crude medicine
The pigskin's deep ᵹᴀe boLᵹᴀ shag
Right through the Doire air and in
Cú Chulainn's colon enema
Expels his alien enemy.

Propels it up and out his gob
Above Srath Mór it hurtles north
Where into Eagle's Rock it's lob
Smashes it with loud report
Cú Chulainn too is lifted off
To land him up Dún Leochain way
His ass well kicked and right ticked off
At Móin na nIonadh games they play
Though Fionn declares the match a draw
Conditions were so wild in Straw.

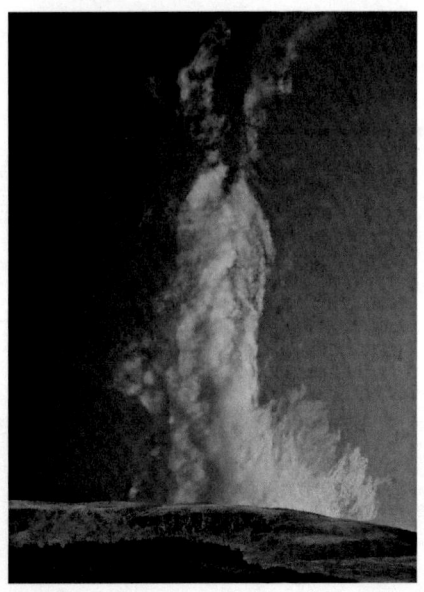

4. hÚdaigh's Uaes

It's fortunate Dún Leochain sports
A healthy wee distillery
For Cú Chulainn now so out of sorts
Will need to drown his misery
The druid wife of Muireadh there
Hospitable and shrewd
Concocts an Úr from heather rare
That's sure to change Cú Chulainn's mood
For moss and air on Spelhoagh's steep slope
Uplifts the most dejected mope.

When she heard Cú Chulainn splash
Some time before the crack of dawn
She rose and brewed a goodly stash
And took it through the rain   still on
To where our hero lay on Spelhoagh
A soggy sight   sore waterlogged
Feelin mighty sorry for himself
Up to his eyes half-drowned and bogged
And all around him half asleep
A hundred head of curious sheep.

Him countin them to stay awake
Them ruminatin on this sight
Him sinkin in a mossy lake
Them unconcerned about his plight
So to his rescue and relief
The druidess pours down his throat
Úr good brown tae it's her belief
Will buoy him up and make him float
And sure enough he starts to rise
Till up above the bog he flies.

The sheep alarmed take off and flee
In all directions through the moss
The good shepherd he tries to be
But in the mist they've all been lost
Time too is lost and runnin out
Untethered in this sunless space
So shades who shouldn't be about
But are and do come face to face
With Cú Chulainn in Úr trance
And one stands out and not by chance.

A shepherd and dindseanachie
Who knows these wile and woolly lands
And elder of Clan Cinneididh
Once used to ewes and rams and lambs
He gives Cú Chulainn sage advice
And tips on where to find lost sheep
By namin' mountain lands precise
Locations he could walk in sleep
Spellin out the spots round Spelhoagh
Where a sheep might stop and find itself.

Says he, *"Try Liggiariagh*
Or Glenarum or Benroonaigh
Face of the Park or Altalavragh
Gulliamuck or Gulliacrevaigh
Or even Moneywillyglen.
They might be out by Shiskin way
Or up Craigbane or Fionnaglen
In Gulliaharig or Boich Brae."
So when he searches Fionnaglen
Cú Chulainn there finds Fionn again.

They rounded up a wheen more sheep
But two wee lambs cud not be found
Without the patience of Bo Peep
Until they hear a Mantic sound
That caused a tip and ewe to bleat

By Ranaghan the sound increased
To Elemental Zealous beat
Whose Coda shook both man and beast
Ahead they saw a Barefoot crowd
Enraptured by a music loud.

There in among a dancin throng
The lambs lepped round with Little Hooks.
What was this ꝼleaḋh of dance and song
Where Eagle's Rock here overlooks?
Cú Chulainn would interrogate
What is this lunacy of noise?
This Mojo Fury Immediate
That has me Ego lossin poise?
That makes me mind a Fractured Zoo
A General Fiasco too?

'Dancin at Lughnasa' says Fionn
'It must be what that Leaba man
Back there told us we should take in
So let's enjoy it while we can.'
The real truth was that they were still
In the Clutch of wine Elation
Free Riders now to Hy Brasil
Reachin eagle elevation
Where bands of Screaming Gypsies flew
As Hams and witches soared on Q.

The Moin Na Nionadh Undertones
Of deep Red Organ Serpent Sound
Echo Nice 'n' Sleazy from the stones
Of Craig na Shoke above the ground
Where The Tides of SuperFreakz
Like Díseart Hearts in Deep Fried Funk
A Farago of Jaws that speaks
In Cat Malojian Sword Chant punk
Beat Poets Fighting With the Wire
Spout fountain rime In Case of Fire.

Our heroes both in Alpha States
To Scary Bits cuts cut away
Cú Chulainn sees their Black Horse fates
Black Tokens of Omega day
Fionn sees in Coma   King   Ard Ri
Through the looking Glass   go bury
His true love Grainne in the lee
Of Mullagh Mór's Indigo Fury.
And Fionn mere low civilian
Can only watch the Triggerman.

'Here Come the Landed Gentry Kings
Of Chadsko, Troy and Panama
They bring the eXtra offerings
Of Lotion myrrh for Savasana
And So I Watch You From Afar
La Faro way you've gone mo Grainne
Self Healer though you think you are
My Open eye myrrh sees upOn ya
So now you've crossed the Dell aware
Of Swanny River Stix down there.'

And like the first damned Angel Fall
The tides of time's Ignition flash
MeFisto makes his collect call
And nothin but The Rags and Ash
Remain like Skruff on this redoubt
Silence returns to Eagle's Rock
Red Sirus Jaded Sun burnt out
Lambs re-enfolded in the flock
Maigh dTamlacht forests yield to gloom
And stars their shiftin shape resume.

When mornin sun lights up the Rock
Our heroes stir beneath its cliff
Awakened by the strangest cock
That ever cocked a doodle riff
For up there on the precipice
There flapped an eagle? bat-man? owl?
Prepared to launch into abyss
With boords for wings and tail of fowl
From off two dozen ganders' wings
Tied tight with bog oak sliver strings.

'What bird is this?' Cú Chulainn says
What hybrid birdbrain have we here?'
'It's must be hÚdaigh of the Uaes
Says Fionn 'A wild Mag Uiginn I fear
Who rides the bulls and leps the nags
And now it looks as if he plans
To fly off Craig na Shoke's high crags
Is that you, hÚdaigh?!' Fionn demands
His echoed shout bounced off the Rock
'Come down off there you mad half-cock!'

The answer from this chanticleer
A loud shrill crow back down he hurled
'I am the bravest chevalier
That ever was in all the world
I aim to fly across the foam
To Beinn Nibheis the highest peak
Up there I'll rest and then fly home
So in the future men will speak
Of hÚdaigh as a shinin' knight
Who lek an eagle soared in flight.'

'Take it aesey yet ye eejet bat!'
Fionn calls up, "Even I would
Not try an aerie feat like that
Yer nutts to fly before ye should
Be me eye I see an alder grove
Over thonder ye might fly there
But my advice before ye rove
With boords for wings is don't trust aer
Aer aren't what ye think it is
You'll fall in Dún before you've riz!'

Cú Chulainn calls a warnin too
"Don't be a quarter clift birdman!"
But undeterred the eejet flew
And glided like a pelican
At first it seems he's got it right
Circlin out Dunmurry way
Him squakin on his maiden flight
A song of glee and liberty
"O, I have the wings of a swallow
And I will fly over the sea ..."

But this hubristic attitude
Would aviation gods displease
He starts to lose his altitude
His flappin boords begin to freeze
Goose feathers loosen as he flaps
He plunges headlong towards the trees
And into Crocawillia draps
The Srath Mór bird brought to his knees
Our heroes to the rescue bound
To where poor hÚdaigh hits the ground.

A crumpled heap the find him snared
Among the brambles ripped and torn
Wan leg broken   thigh bone bared
His flying future now forlorn
But local druid Feidhlidh comes
And splints him up and offers drink
'Will ye have a Crock? This here rum's
The boy to get ye in the pink.'
'I will'   groans hÚdaigh 'take a drap
But jist this wance for my mishap.'

'This here Crock o Willow Sail'
Says hÚdaigh   now uplifted high
'Has towl to me the morra's tale
Of sallyin the silent skiy
To live at aese at its expense
Flyin's ony for the birds'   says he
'Unless ye do it in a sense
Av sel ris up and flyin free
Ye are the birds an clouds immense
All wan wi ye   no difference.'

'When I was up there sailin round
A wee bird lit on my owl head
And sang a song   a wile sad sound
That towl me of a time of dread
When foul air scunners all that flies
So full it is of soot and shite
From fartin flyin fools half-wise
Who cannot thole for wan fortnight
Their own townland   their own fouled nest
With their birdsong no longer blest.'

'They'll fly for fun   full filled with fuel
Black lard of baests from long ago
The smoke and reek of fire cruel
Lettin off a haeted glow
That cowps the way the clouds are cast
So druth and drinch are double due
And faest and famish folly fast
To waste our waens and their waens too
And turn me lovely owl Srath Mór
To livin hell from heaven's door.'

II

'The clift's half wise'   we'll take him home
Says Fionn   'We'll lift him time about
Come on   ye boy ye   up ye come
Brave man ye are   we'll help ye out
When your mad flight is wisely seen
Some day your name will show the way
Through glens and moss of widest Screen
Where them who wander want to stay
In their own land that gave them birth
To see its beauty and its worth.'

By way of Doire an Fhoid they hod
Limp hÚdaigh   hoisted shoulder high
Until they reach that oakwood sod
That blocks the view of mount and sky
Where druid Dochartaigh's rare Dair
From rural woods that there abound
Makes drinkers' heads as light as air
Up in the clouds that rowl around
The never restin crest they seek
Great Mullagh Mór   Screen's highest peak.

The pioneer of man-powered flight
Breaks his pledge just one more time
And from his Dair borne lofty height
Crows down upon the Screen sublime
'It's Grey Goose feathers make me go
And Redbreast Rooster Famous Grouse
Wild Turkey too and thon Oul Crow
Rid Speckled Hen and wee titmouse.'
Our heroes quell his fly man roar
And hod him home to sweet Srath Mór .

hÚdaigh seen to   our heroes climb
Back up the steep Dún Muiri way
And in the fort there spend some time
Quaffin druid Muireadh's tae.
Which sends them on their way to Cluain
Well fortified to replicate
Themselves both skin and bone
Shape shiftin now   multiplicate
For in the depth of dark Cluain wood
No one   alone   should dare intrude.

46

5. Moyola Maes

Each tree within looks just the same
Each branch and twig and leaf alike
So in the gloom its claim to fame
Is   all who enter   terrors strike
For one is lost here right away
Unless oneself one multiplies
By five or ten or twenty   say
The only way survival lies
Enough of one to go around
One self lost will soon be found.

Soon enough Fionn's seeing double
Two Cú Chulainns   three   then four
As he himself thinks they're in trouble
Self replicatin more and more
Till all the way for five miles straight
An army forms of ranks of Fionn
And hosts of his Cú Chulainn mate
For each a universe within
In parallel this multitude
Now swarms the trees of Cluain Wood.

╫

One problem now with this cute trick
Is pulling selves together right
After such arithmetic
It's solved again by getting tight

So all the selves must then imbibe
The Onn of Cluain from sap of ash
Distilled by druids of the tribe
Of Liam   to an oily mash
That gives the scattered selves a lift
So back together all shapes shift.

Both reunited once again
Beyond the symmetrees of Cluain
They meet Ceathru na Móna men
Gathered round a towerin stone
On which is writ an Ogham text
A message quare mysterious
That has those gathered there perplexed
'It's changin and aethereous'
Says one of these cool citizens
The townland's druid denizens.

Our Fionn's a skilled decipherer
Of signs in code or runic marks
But this one is much stifferer
Seems made of light that waves and sparks
With shiftin forms that won't him free
To give him time to find the key
That might   unlock the mystery
'It's lek a trick of light ye see
It's lek thon lightnin up in Straw
Says Fionn   'that on the field of play we saw.'

47

⏤⏤ IIIII

From deep within the stone recessed
They draw out drams of fruitful drink
Concoctions made from apple pressed
'The apple of yer i   I think'
Says one and offers it to Fionn
*'This Ceirt will be your eyes and ears
Transportin you without and in
So near and far the same appears
Bell fast   not slow   down dell   up hill
Fly well beyond the Mercmobille*

*'And as for young Cú Chulainn   you
Partake of this blackberry Pin
From bushes down by Mullán a Mhú
And though it will not change your scene
You'll know the mind of your friend Fionn
You'll see and hear his every thought
Though he in distant orbits spin
Yer thumbs will find this cosmonaut
And if at first ye don't connect
Re search in motion will correct.'*

⏤⏤ ///

One ruddy draught and Fionn's away
He hops right into Baile na nIúr
Skips Maigh na gCuigeadh   Gort na Sceach
Leps Dún Tí Bhriain on his tour
Up through thin Stragh Mountain air
And lands on high Sliabh Gallon peak
All along the watchtower there
Yet to Cú Chulainn still can speak
Though distanced by a broad domain
Across Moyola's lovely plain.

Cú Chulainn's call   Fionn clearly hears
His message is   *'G'wan   g'wan'*
But Fionn's in awe of what appears
Eastward from the peak he's on
The wide expanse of brilliant light
That is Loch nEeathach in bright sunshine
And there   at berth   a rarer sight
A sailin ship at its shoreline
'My ship'   a voice behind him says
Fionn spins to meet a stranger's gaze.

A weathered face from wind and sun
A salt-sea sailor without doubt
Fionn greets the dark and wanderin one
An argonaut who'd voyaged out
From fabled sunburnt land of Greece
And somehow found himself in Screen
'I'm searching for the Golden Fleece
But heard in Gaul of this   'pot een?'
Made only on this far-flung isle
And by the gallon here   in style.'

'Aye   right ye be'   says Fionn   'It's true
This is the very place right here
I'll lead you to Stragh Mountain Dew
Of son of Taidgh   the druid seer
The golden fleece may be a prize
Worth the risky voyage here
But pulls the wool about yer eyes
Unlike our spirits crystal clear
For Taidgh's elixir's golden   bright
And he won't fleece ye when yer tight.'

Before they reach Taidgh's neighbourhood
Cú Chulainn calls demanding news
He might be missin something good
Like some new mind-expandin booze
So when he hears of Grecian quest
He leps across Moyola's vale
To meet this famed heroic guest
At whom at first he'll rant and rail
But when he hears the sailor's tales
He's quare impressed   good sense prevails.

The trio then commence to sip
Taidgh's Stragh Mountain Golden Coll
That lets imagination rip
With tales fantastical and tall
The Greek has stories of his trip
Of hydras harpies   horrid beasts
And gods that nearly wrecked his ship
Fionn can match these yarns with feats
Of magic   wisdom and romance
Both leave Cú Chulainn in a trance.

His own adventures lack these charms
His stories filled with battle strife
Brute force of might and clash of arms
A bloody Morrigan led life
But spirits soothe the savage heart
He loosens up   remembers Eimear
Recalls her beauty   grace and art
Reveals his soul   the hidden dreamer
They reminisce all through the night
Till mornin bathes the Screen in light.

The Greek should now be on his way
But finds the Screen a tender trap
When in Cath Oir he's wont to stay
To try it's Oir   at least a drap
'I'll put the golden fleece on hold
This place has alchemists of note
Can turn the fruits of earth to gold
What need have I of sheepskin coat?
This place is comin down with stills
There's liquid gold in them there hills.'

His song rings out across the Screen
And down the centuries of time
When mighty clerics rule the scene
Whose callins misconstrue the rhyme
Thinkin riches can be found
Beneath Sliabh Gallon's purple sage
If foreign miners dig the ground
And usher in a Golden Age
Base Sperrin metals would be cast
But dreams of gold would last and last.

And Fionn now sees the Greek anew
Could this boy be his son   Oisín?
Shape shifted through the golden brew
Returned from Tír na nÓg unseen?
His wanderin in some time warp
Not recognizin home or da?
So changed is he by Niamh's harp
Her voice the Sirens' orchestra?
His fallin off his horse a tale
To steer his father off the trail?

Fionn keeps his thoughts close to his vest
His dear doe love best kept untold
But now that Jason's drunk the best
Fionn says to this young hero bold
'Now that you've imbibed in Screen
An honour we   on you   bestow
From here on in your name's Oisín
So all you meet where we now go
Will know how time can be reversed
And rhyme inverse in feet rehearsed.'

Jason Oisín on his sea legs
Rollin   tackin   undulatin
Through six townlands on shaeky pegs
With Fionn amused and navigatin
Along the Alt na Goan stream
And into verdant Gort na Sceach
Where druid Coill Mór traps the steam
Of hawthom Uath's fine uisce
Inducin visions in these three
Of mighty dragons yet to be.

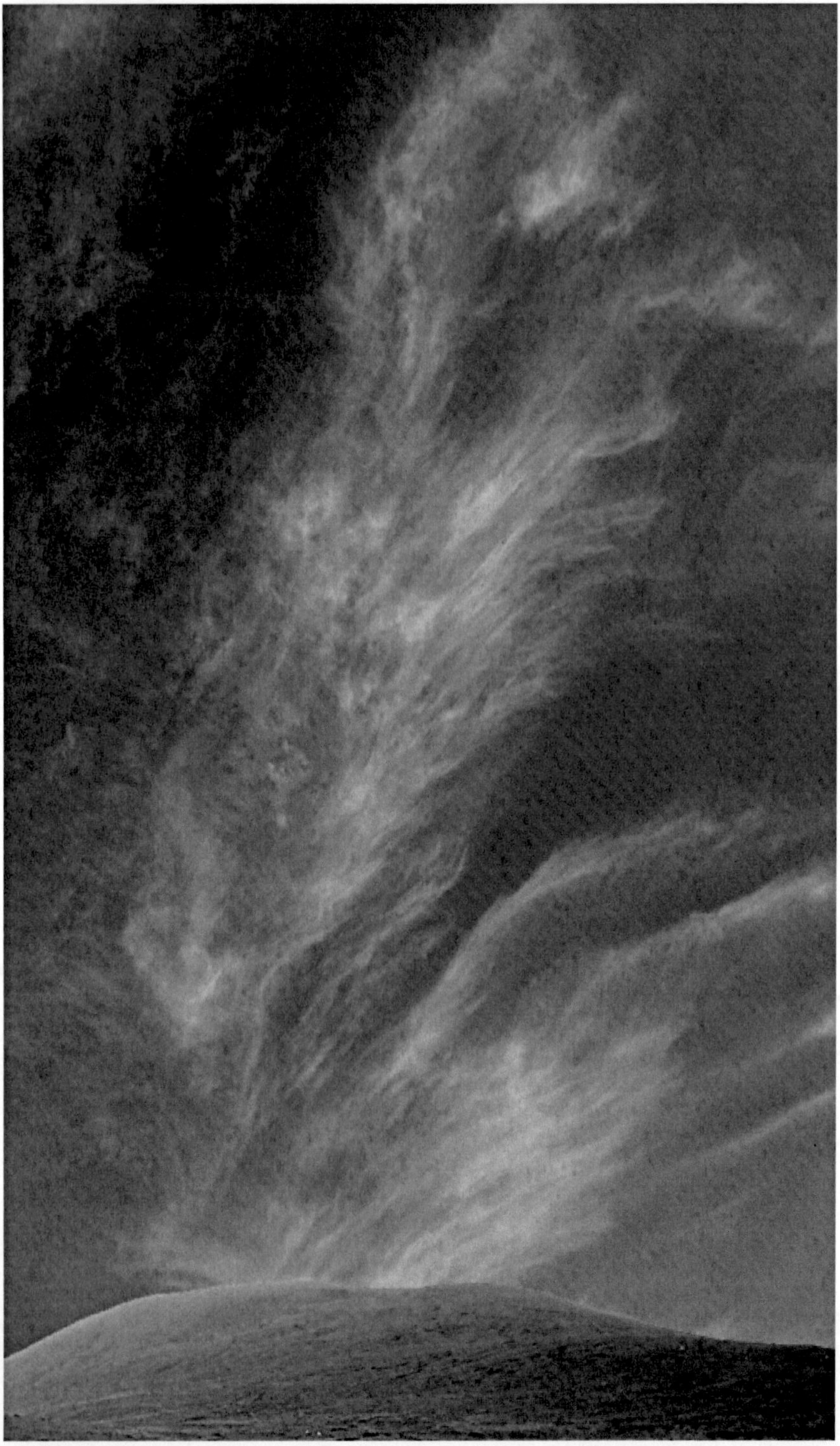

For as they journey on the path
The very ground begins to shake
And in their ears a roarin wrath
Of some approachin monstrous snake.
Right near a dwellin up ahead
A wooden gate now bars the way
But over this Cú Chulainn sped
Intent on enterin the fray
Though when he sees the baest advance
He thinks he hasn't got a chance.

Belchin smoke and streamin vapour
The monster charges blindly on
Cú Chulainn   like a matador
Steps aside and then it's gone
Though not before he sees its gut
Filled with victims of its greed.
Then from near the dwellin hut
A witness to Cú Chulainn's deed
'In all the years as sairgeant here
I've never seen a deed so queer.'

'What sort of man are ye at all
Would go agin a thing like that?'
'I thought your hut would surely fall
Be crushed and smashed and baeten flat.'
'Begod you are both thick and brave
Come in and bring your friends with you
And have a drap before you laev
Of Gort na Sceach's Gort Uath dew.
You'll meet the chariot bubble man
And seamstress of the Bloscadh clan."

Well-ceilied there   they head on o'er
Owl Banty bridge in Glebe townland
Where once again a thunderin roar
Greets our misty wandrin band
This time it's from a clear blue sky
From which a great   loud bird swoops down
Landin on a field nearby
And on its back a man seems bound
'A harpy   here?'   the Greek cries out
Says Fionn   'A loutish hÚdaigh   I doubt.'

'I say   I say'   this birdman squawks
'What have we here on our estate?
A gang of Shinners out for walks?
Trespassing we'll not tolerate!
I fought the Huns in desert sands
To free us from the likes of you!
Be off with you   from these our lands.'
The trio shocked at this cuckoo
Decide a lesson might be due
Respondin to his cry and hue.

Such coorse welcome irks Cú Chulainn
His wild is up   can hardly spaek
Except in grunts both crude and sullen
'Yer wings need clippin   and yer baek.'
With that he snaps off both the wings
And rips the cock from out his pit
Yanks the whurlin nose and flings
It   wings and man   the whole outfit
Through Cnoc Dubh skies the bits all soar
Crash landin deep in Tobair Mór.

The Greek`s amazed at this event
'Friend Heracles would be impressed.'
Cú Chulainn now his ragin' spent
Dismisses praise and quickly stressed
'Thon sort of thing just gets me riled
His welcome was despicable
This land may be a wee bit wild
But Uladh is hospitable
His arrogance alone reveals
He is no marshal of these fields.'

|||| ̅6̅

Glebe's reputation now is healed
By small Iodhadh brewed from yew
When grand big dwellin near the field
Gives them a holt on this fine dew
To set them up for Dún Tí Bhriain
The land of Clandeboye UiNeill
Whose fort is famed for Uileann wine
And feast of Bann-caught Toomebridge eel
To which they are invited now
Since news has spread of their Glebe row.

They're greeted warmly by UiNeill
Brian Carrach holding court
But Fionn's suspicious of his zeal
Knowin that he stole this fort
From Cadhan tribes who'd long been here
By ruthless underhanded schemes
And sure enough his gut felt fear
Is soon confirmed by shouts and screams
As guards attack the friendly Greek
For savage sport this chief will seek.

It seems when Brian hangs a man
He likes to see a couple dance
So anyone from any clan
Will hang   who happens there by chance
So here's this foreigner will do
To get his gallows quota up
This Brian knows a thing or two
He gets Cú Chulainn first to sup
The Micigh Fionn spiked cup of Uileann
So there   knocked out   lies boul Cú Chulainn.

So Fionn's alone agin a hundred
But nothin fazes our McCumhaill
He soon has Brian Carrach scunnered
Though not an aesy man to fool.
'Yer in for one god awful shock
This Greek will be the death of you
His ship is sailin from the lough
Manned by wan almighty crew
His first mate   mighty Heracles
Who'll crush a hundred men with aese.'

Brian's heard of Heracles all right
But wonders if McCumhaill is bluffin
Says Fionn   *'I hear he loves to fight*
I hear he`s knocked the stuffin
Out of every strongman worth his salt
From Antrim   Portglenone and Toome
And now he says he will not halt
Till Brian Carrach meets his doom
We came here to help you   Brian
We're phucht with big Cú Chulainn lyin.'

UiNeill who doesn't often panic
Now goes berserk at Fionn's big lie
He drives his druid nearly manic
To brew a drink to rectify
The stupour of Cú Chulainn's swoon
Little knowin Heracles is stuck
Down in deepest Fallaghgloon
Where Sirens from round Lisnamuck
Seduce him with their pulchritude
And have him dancin jigs so lewd.

52

The druid soon revives Cú Chulainn
Who gets the picture right away
He boots uiNeill to far Glenullin
And frees the Greek without delay
They head for Móin na gCuigeadh's hills
The first of these ... Cnoc na Dair Dubh
Boasts a plethora of stills
And black oak casks to age the dew
The Dairest dew that`s ere distilled
In Doire's dewlapped dales fulfilled.

It's here in this transition zone
Between the Planter and the Gael
Opposin gods as one are shown
Imbibin from the self same grail
Where foolish fights fought over faith
Are fast forgotten   forced afar
By fine fermented Dair and Beith
From fulsome   fruitful   fulfilled jar
Of blackest black hill black oak booze
And whitest Whitefort rowan Luis.

The fields are fired with orange blaze
Surrounded by the verdant green
Our trio drinks the many ways
That harmonies suffuse the Screen
They hear the tones those Hannas sing
In praise of spirits they revere
And how the Forge's anvils ring
To arm with pike the volunteer
Who tyranny would bravely fight
And with another faith unite.

They hear the Wolf call loud and clear
A call to freedom from the gods
Who manacle the mind with fear
Dividin neighbours set at odds
But then they see the wolf's extinct
The justice gone from nature's scales
And only in this vale distinct
Is any hope that peace prevails
When men together share the dew
Derived from bounty nature grew.

Cú Chulainn feels the wolf loss most
Regrets the times he slaughtered it
Sees how much it was our host
Invitin us to live with it
Allowin it some space at least
And show us balance is the key
Equality for man and beast
But lord protectors could not see
Beyond their petty deities
To how and what the wolf kind sees.

And drink they do without a care
Until they drink the townland dry
But now the Greek becomes aware
That he might have to say goodbye
To Screen and drink and new-found friends
For as they look towards Milltown race
They see a sail come round the bends
Of deep Moyola's current pace
With   floatin there   above the prow
Heracles   luckin for a row?

This Heracles seems slightly frail
A shadow of the legend told
But noble   proud and in full sail
His look is wise and strong and bold
And from his tongue trail light   fine chains
Each one a link to those below
Whose ears are held as if by reins
That lead them on   all pleased to go
Wherever he decides and deigns
Hangin on his long   loquacious   fluent strains.

Says he to Fionn   'What are these brutes
So hugely clad in armoured suits
That roar around this land in boots
That tear the very soil and roots
Of all that grows in this green vale
And smell like burning beastly flesh
That fouls the air in which I sail
So men don't feel the winds afresh
Or hear bird songs in chorus mesh
Slick Trojan Horses filled with Greeks
Bearing gifts with fetid breath and oily reeks?"

Fionn wonders what is goin' on
First Oisín   an argonaut?
Now Heracles   a changed icon?
No giant frame   more finely wrought
A man of words   not swords   more wise
With an air of strong conviction
Shapeshiftin Oghma   in disguise?
Oisín sees friend   Fionn's transfixion
Says he   'Don't be deceived by size
He's Ogmios of eloquence when thus he flies.'

Cú Chulainn's stunned by what he sees
Not all that big compared to him
But all his recent mellow ease
Seems now abruptly but a whim
They eye each other head to toe
Circlin   wary   calculatin
But Fionn and Oisín   they both know
A bit of good intoxicatin
Might loosen up the tension taut
With which this mighty standoff's fraught.

6. Cross Fair Daes

'Come on now lads   lets have drink
Maigh Chaolain Uillean is the best
Bendin your elbows   don't you think
Will help to soothe the savage breast?'
The champions finally simmer down
And with reluctance do proceed
To bochaR buí   the Cross's town
Where Mercmobilles in masses speed
But there they find a waterin hole
The very place that was Fionn's goal.

For here is found the very fount
Of why An Scrín is to the fore.
At least a score of druids count
Maigh Chaolain   Maigh Chaorthain and Cath Oir
The single greatest concentration
Of highly skilled practitioners
In the arts of fermentation
And spirit distillation wares
They say all roads do lead to Rome
But round this Cross is spirit's home.

Mac Cionnadha's is a druid lair
It's been for generations long
A spot for travelers to repair
Who've reached tracks end to sit among
The native characters of note
From ancient Broin and Ceallach clan
Who clothed and fed this land remote
But now horse huaisle to a man
Quaffin beverages and wine
And tellin fondly yarns equine.

Here Cú Chulainn stabilises
Entranced by tales of horses swift
As is Heracles* who prizes
Steeds with spirit that can shift
So these two now like long lost mates
Share the crack on the sport of kings
But drink and crack accelerates
Their need for speedy conquerins
Nag braggin rights must now be claimed
Competition's fires inflamed.

* Heracles referred to as "Oghma" from this point on.

Cú Chulainn whistles loud and long
And soon his trusty Laeg appears
With stallion Liath Macha strong
While Oghma calls his charioteers
From far Olympus where the gods
Send Pegasus the flying steed
That's guaranteed to beat the odds
Even agin an Irish breed
The course is set   agin the law
To hell and back   by way of Straw.

||||

First to SeanSeo's Maigh Chaorthain still
Where bets are placed of one to two
Despite Cú Chulainn`s riding skill
That he will lose when race is through
'What odds? says he   'I'll baet the bum
To hell and back's a long   long way
And since he's got a horse to come
With wings   nigh hell he'll niver neigh
So give us   SeanSeo   your fleet footed sup
Fresh alder Fearn to fasten us up.'

'It's all about reason changin the rhyme
To shatter the myths of space and time
That Oghma eejit hasn't a clue
He thinks there's a Hades (most of them do)
He can fly all day on Pegasus' back
But he won't get there   so he won't get back
When ye take the oul yarns like the one I'm in now
And see them as real and true somehow
Ye've abandoned what's plainly in front of yer eyes
This Heracles Oghma's only half wise.'

||||

While still in Maigh Chaorthain they must go off course
To the house of MacMaolain to fit out each horse
As felicitous a man as ever you'd meet
Who soon has them girdled and saddled complete
'Come on'   says MacCumhaill   *'We've plenty of time*
We'll call with MacConmhaoil for beverage sublime
For Mac na Midhe mead from Maigh Chaorthain hives
Will reverse the Míls for the race of our lives.'
So there at the corner   luckin out on The Cross
They drink and discuss who has the best hoss.

####

By the time they are done the horses need food
So back to Maigh Chaolain for a long interlude
At the house of a Ceallach who thrashes wild oats
To brew up a stout to soothe their parched throats
You can bank on this Donnchadha to feed horse and man
And pass on his secrets to the Dearg Domhnall clan
Whose Straif of Blackthorn   steeple chaser delight
Should be supped on the stoop till your nearly half tight
Through a sunlit split Diamint they all take their fill
While watchin the sport on the village Fair Hill.

There come the young bucks from all local clans
Mac Uiginns   Mac hAllions and them Ceallach wans
To play foreign games with the ball and the bat
Though   if The Boss is about   to hide what they're at
With all this distraction   the horse race delayed
And a visit to Muireadh's now must be paid
Where the druidess   Moll   the Siren of hosts
Adept at the hanlin of men full of boasts
Sets fondly her eyes on these warriors four
To welcome them warm near that meetin house door.

┼

    She plies them with Muin   the mellowest brew
    Certain to soothe an obstreperous crew
    So now even Oghma is gettin laed back
    Postponin the rally   enjoyin the crack.
Though he's come through a hot Bacchanalian clime
He's shocked by these brews and how they change time
    How he finds himself then   and then he's here now
    How sometimes he's not but doesn't know how
    His labours seem pointless his dozen or so
When you don't know the morra from long   long ago.

┼

    None of the rest are any more knowin
    About whether they're gone or comin or goin'
    For they find themselves now with Cadhan the Druid
    Whose alchemist's skill turns Ailm to a fluid
    Inflamin their passions that nearly had died
    With well prescribed potions only he can provide
    Handed down by MacLiam   Maolain and Tomhnair
Whose concoctions will cure what ails an oul boner
So now the two boyos are wild   rampant hallions
    More taken with fillies than racin' their stallions.

    And wouldn't you know it   as darkness falls
    The village is filled with lovely young dolls
    Dickied up   sweet smellin   lookin divine
    Headin up Cath Oir lane where stars brightly shine
    And The Screen comes alive with a heavenly dance
    Of adventure and horror and   of course   romance
    While there at the back of a starstruck crowd
    Sit our heroes applaudin the action out loud
Says Oisín   'Back home   'it's the same screen we crave
    The same bright illusion in wise Plato's cave.'

    The magi MacUiginns   bringers of light
    Are floodin the Screen with images bright
    Then sons of the Maolain clan carry the flame
    To fill fickle minds with flickerin fame
    With tall   timeless tales from places exotic
    Of heroes enamoured by damsels erotic
    And there in the dark when a kiss is bestowed
    There's mass imitation of what's bein' showed
    And if there's a battle or duel or fight
    Makin' wans like MacGothraidh yell with delight.

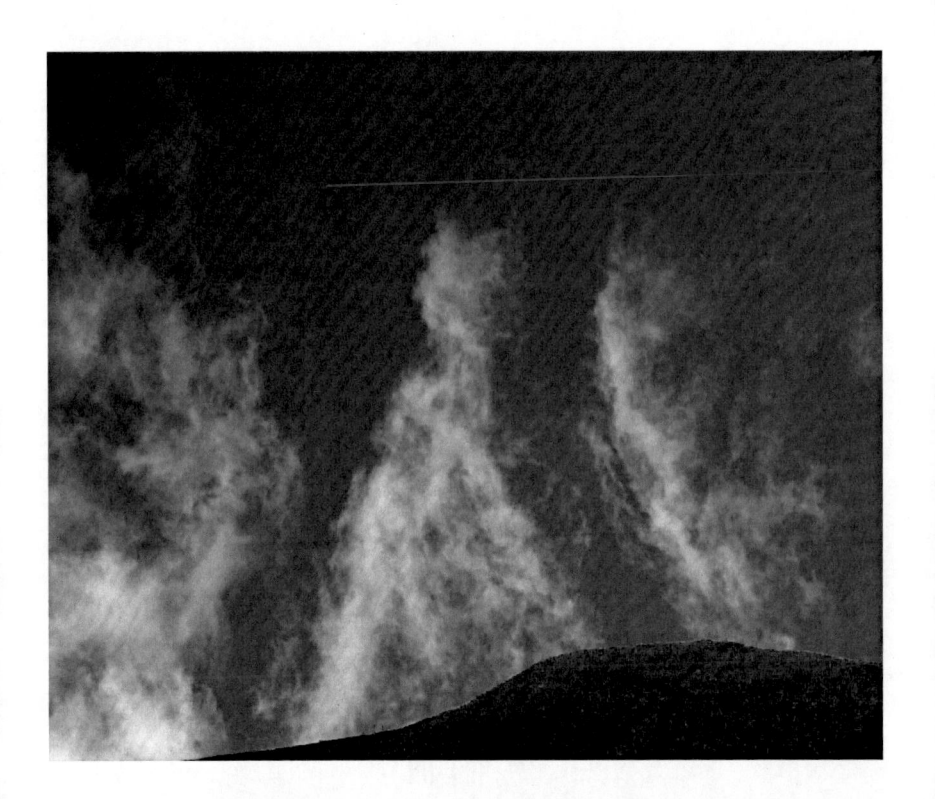

'I've a gra for the weemin up in the oul Screen'
Says Cú Chulainn   'the loveliest I've seen
With their eyes always dancin and taekin ye in
You'd think they were goddesses livin in sin
They're wile for the ride   on the oul chariot
And they always will give as good as they got
Sure   all is forgiven when ye do somethin bad
As long as it's a girl from The Screen yev had
No need to repent   it's never obscene
Yer away to the races with a girl from The Screen."

Oghma is snoggin   hearin Cú Chulainn
Takes a wee break from the things he's pullin
Says he   quite indignant 'Ach   go away
The women of Greece   they know how to play
They put on live shows   they're not in your mind
These girls from the Screen   there's nothing behind
They're wispy wee things like nymphets or sprites
I like a woman who'll put out the lights.'
With this his wee Screen woman lands him a right
Near laevin him permanent claen out of sight.

The ructions that follow are hard to describe
There's a wile load of noise   a fierce diatribe
The crowd goes berserk and our boys escape
Back down the lane corner to look for some grape
To the home of the druid known as Ⲧⲁⲣbh
Where no one goes thirsty or is likely to starve
There Oghma with shiner lets out a roar
Demandin the wine of local Cath Oir
'Don't rile up Ⲁn Ⲧⲁⲣbh'   says Fionn to the Greek
'Or it's havoc on us   he's likely to wreak.'

When Ⲁn Ⲧⲁⲣbh appears there isn't much doubt
This incredible hulk could take them all out.
Says he   'It's not nice to be gulderin so
So wheesht or it's out on yer arse ye'll go.
If yer lookin for Or   the kettle is dry
But I have Gaulish wine ye might want to try.'
'Be Zeus that'll do' says Oghma now
Feelin chastised for his ignorant row
The new wine is shown   'How about this?
I'm toul it's the best of bó Ʒeⲁlous Ⲡⲓs.'

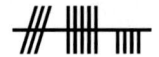

𝍫 𝍪 𝍨

And so would begin   one very strange night
Dionysian wild till dawn's early light
With Ⲡⲓs toper folk all spaekin in tongues
Shoutin and singin at the top of their lungs
While slip disc go dancin and head bangin din
Has the village in uproar   its head in a spin.
This corner goes mad at the foot of The Cross
And it's not plaesin some   especially The Boss
With Whom even Ⲁn Ⲧⲁⲣbh will not lock horns
Don't want to cross Him   He's a real crown of thorns.

You're busted in the blindin lights   it's closin time
If you're not soon out of there   it's a crime
But The Boss don't like these dizzy heights
That's why He blinds with his blindin lights
So the fearsome four bid fond farewell
To Ⲁn Ⲧⲁⲣbh and the Ⲡⲓs and the fear of hell
That The Boss of The Cross has instilled in all
And still is instillin   though distillin it small
But across The Cross   they hear the first bar
Of 'Drop kick me   GAA Zeus   right Over The Bar.'

While crossin The Cross   they nearly get hit
By a hoss and a cart with The Boss drivin it
'No crossing The Cross'   roars The Boss from on high
'Or I'll bar you for good   on The Cross you will die.'
When you're over The Bar   your point is a Cross
When you're under The Bar   The Cross is The Boss
Don't Cross The Boss for The Bar is too far
That goal isn't in   it hits The Cross Bar
When The Boss is this cross   He'll give you a clout
That'll make your head spin like some round about.

The Boss   a shapeshifter with many a guise
Most of them dark like rooks or black flies
Some sportin hats like the baeks on the birds
Some frocked up in red and not stuck for words
A good many prone to an oul boy aroma
Incensin innocence into a coma
They criss cross the Screen makin' signs for The Cross
Like *'Do this and do thon or your soul you will loss.'*
White torques and tonsures in habit the scene
With bell   book and coinneal they're rookin the Screen.

Says Oisín to Fionn   *'This Boss is a cuss*
I'm not puttin up with this bossin of us
Hi Boss Basileus   on your hoss and cart
You near run us down and that isn't smart.'
And Oghma is thinkin there might be a case
For The Boss to get left with egg on his face
'A warnin'   says Fionn   *'If you egg on The Boss*
He'll fry you for breakfast and not give a toss
No sunny side up   he can't take a joke
Hard-boiled or scrammled   he's a terrible yolk.'

⋈

From here they can smell wile strong Seamróg Tae
For the down under Ceallach   an outlaw they say
Has recipes passed by Mac Na Midhe clan
Sharp Pin pointed potions to place kick a man
A boot to the balls was never so sore
As partin the posts with this winnin score
The Donnghailes too have their part in the play
In pullin big points   though not for much pay
'When you're lossin the game through trouble and strife
Drop kick me Gruagain through the goalposts of life.'

61

Well oiled and flush they take a few strides
To find themselves where Clan Riagan presides
A long line of druids steeped deep in the past
All partial to potables packin a blast
Of all the purveyors of potion and beef
They rose to the top   these druids in chief
With so many drinkers downin their drams
They made a wild killin   bendin Uillean and hams
So there by the sound of The Shammel's loud moo
Our heroes are welcomed to partake of the dew.

The Ceallachs   the Cadhans   the hUidhrins here
The Brollaghans   the MacAodahas often appear
MacUiginns   Donnghailes   all of these clanns
Frequent these Shammels in large caravans
They have much in common besides Riagain drinks
With a grá for oul music and keepin the links
A good many past it   though all young at heart
They keep the place hoppin   all play their part
This might be the centre   the heart of The Screen
Where clanns mingle freely to take in the scene.

One of the drinkers stands out from the rest
A big fella   Cadhan   with zest for the jest
And an uncanny knack of killin the time
By sconchin all round him in scurrilous rhyme
When he sees the four strangers his eyes are lit up
He can't miss the chance of a good oul cutup
So he launches a salvo directed at Fionn
About how he loved Grainne but couldn't get in
And then at Cú Chulainn about his wee size
And how everyone round him gets bolgaed and dies.

Not too long ago this slaggin in rhyme
Would have struck Cú Chulainn as personal crime
He'd have had a warp spasm right out of his mind
And rammed the ᵹáe boLᵹa up Cadhan's behind
But not anymore since findin his tongue
Thanks to Screen Spirit he's not so high strung
And as for the Greeks   they crave a good pome
Sure this boy's a Homer away from their home
And even though Cadhan starts in on them too
They love every word of his rowdy dow do.

They don't have a clue what he's sayin half time
But they like how he spouts it in rough ready rhyme
The insults are flyin about how the Greeks
Put up with foolosophers who fancy lads' cheeks
About how their top doGs like foolin around
And how their economy's runnin aground
With the Greeks well sconched he starts his report
In jest at The Screen for some local sport
For many round here have Olympian dreams
Of competin   defeatin and cheatin on teams.

Says he   'Some of the punters partakin herein
Really lek praetin about puntin pigskin
But most of these clans prefer the oul club
They swing about madly with many a flub
Some take it wile serious   get very teedoff
A ceallach might kill ye if ye even cough
If a bystander happens to utter a sound
He risks being clubbed right into the ground
They want their wee balls to sink in a hole
Though not right away   they lek a good stroll.

They love the oul foreplay   can't get enough
Big head on the shaft to drop to the rough
The swingers of old were fond of the woods
Now iron age clubs deliver the goods
They linger in vales and lap up the hills
Love of trimmed nature gives them their thrills
A good firm hoult of the shaft is a must
You don't want to loss it all in a bust
When your balls get snagged in rough underbrush
By slicin and killin the bird in the bush.

*It's all about gettin your balls to the mound
Where the goin' is soft   nice   smooth and round
Where the dew of the mornin sits on the grass
Your balls get a wettin as they by the hole pass
It's here that your touch must have the caress
To stroke and to slide with thrustin finesse
The final release   the slow folly through
You're watchin the birdie   a wee kiss'll do
Shoot your club in the air   let out a roarae
Can you now get it up for seventeen more   aeh?*

*At the end of a day these clubbers are baet
So it's off to the druids their druth for to saet
And here at the Shammels they all shoot the crack
About how many balls they each got to whack.'
'By GAA Zeus'   says Oisín   'Very strange talk
About a balls of a way to go for a walk
Nike's Olympus would not recognize
Such custom as this as worth any prize.'
Says Fionn   'You are right   it is very odd
I'm for the camán   this custom's a cod.'*

The new mornin rings with the sound of the birds
Our heroes thank Cadhan for his rhymin words
Bid goodbye to Riagan for his druid care
Go in search of an inn where they might repair
Their needs are soon met across Bothar Buí
At the home of the druid   one Eagartaigh
Who boasts of the finest in beds   food and wine
Though there is a wee snag to do with his sign
Which upsets the Greeks when they see what is says
What in their ancient tongue   'aparo'   conveys.

*'No horse?'   says Oghma   'Doesn't bode well
Where in the hell will Pegasus dwell?'
'It isn't in Greek   it's Latin you see'
Says Fionn   showin off his wide literacy
'Eagartaigh prepares   makes ready   provides
Hospitable digs and for hosses besides
Hoss stable out back through thon entry way
For Liath Macha and Pegasus to hay
Where they will get rest for the morra's big race
While we sup libations to keep up the pace.'*

Eagartaigh gives them his Ebhadh day cap
That first flops them flat in a very deep nap
But soon they inflate with a flatulent snore
For this fiery potion makes floppin men soar
They find themselves floatin far over Screen
Lookin down as they fly at a puzzlin scene
For it's not just a vista of space down below
But that deep view of time they've now come to know
In flat on inflation it's eternity
To see The Moyola as it was and will be.

In daytimin dreamtimin taking them through
To Moyola spirits and druids it knew
Like the Coscrachan men who still can be there
Callin time into space   the when of their where
Like the children of Lir   the Guile Lir   the ganch
And the outspoken sage of the Donghaile branch
Who   at eighty odd years   will raise up his leg
Adjustin his shoon   their attention to beg
Holdin forth on how ships from the land of the Iber
Wrecked   fecked and affect each present imbiber.

Apparo   Moyola   both one and the other
The words flow along with out any bother
The Galicians   the Greeks   the Gaels all agree
They've come to the source and seek it with glee
Moyola gondola aloft in hot air
Transported high by Eagartaigh's fare
Seein comins and goins through trees round The Cross
Through oak and through ash right up to the moss
Through thousands of shades of deep verdant green
Lookin down on the forests of Baile na Scrín.

From high vantage point   a clear view below
Of a wild crowd of baests along the lanes flow
The ways are all clogged with horses and cows
With sheep   goats and men   oul boars and their sows
Headin in droves to the soon crowded Cross
A bustlin affair that won't plaese The Boss
'A Fair Day indeed'   says the druid in flight
For traedin and daelin and drinkin all night.'
This dreamboatin voyage now come to an end
They float o'er the Diamant and slowly descend.

Back down on the sod our heroes proceed
Beyond to the Fair Hill in search of a steed
For Oisín and Fionn to join the horse race
For a four horseman field would quicken the pace
And there a steed pair stood still in a stall
A black and a white   standing many hands tall
Their owner an Owl Boy   a pipe in his gob
Says   *'How much am I bid for this mare and her cob?*
A fine brace of nags who'll labour and run
A team you can trust to get the job done.'

Says Oisín   *'I'll buy but you see I am skint*
Can we do a dael where I work a stint?'
The Owl Boy replies   *'We both stand to gain*
I have stables in Stragh in need of a claen.'
Before Oisín speaks   Fionn draws him aside
For some sage advice he needs to confide
Says he   *'Them stables have not seen a graep*
For two thousand years since Straw took its shape
If you dale wae this boyo's very cute ways
You'll be eyedeep in cac *for the rest of your days.'*

'The Fair Dae's a fiddle'   Fionn fairly fears
'Full of flymen finaeglin financiers
On a Friday Fair Dae   well anything's fair
But more fair to say that fairness is rare
Fair play to fair farmers for faring so far
To be fairly fleeced by an *fairly fly* fear
Sheepmen fleece fairly the way they fleece sheep
The sheep fairly sure the shearing is deep
Cattlemen cut daels the way they do bullocks
Fair slicin and dicin   fair crushin them bollocks.'

But Oghma   he hears and offers a hand
Saying   *'Labours like this I can aesily stand*
No stable or byre's too boggin for me
So tell him we'll do it if he will agree
To advance you the nags to haul the manure
The job'll be done in a day I am sure.'
The Owl Boy suspects connivin's afoot
But four agin wan suggests being cute
Would not be a ploy to put into play
So he ups and agrees to do it their way.

With handspit and slap the bargain is made
'Now who are these nags for which I'll have paid?
What are the names of this gallopin pair?'
'Darcaigh's the stallion   Dollaigh's the mare.'
The Owl Boy says as he bids them farewell
'I'll see you in Stragh   jist folly the smell.'
Now Oisín tells Fionn to pick from the horses
'That's aesy'   says Fionn and quickly endorses
'Darcaigh'   says he   *'He's got mettle and heart.'*
Says Oisín   *'My Dollaigh   bright bán and smart'*

Provisioned   made ready and soundly prepared
Our heroes set out on the way unimpaired
Although they're enlightened   there's heavier tasks
For now they must seek the Underworld casks
And who better guide to this cellar realm
Than a Greek argonaut right strong at the helm?
For once crossed the Stix the sound of the seas
Explodes in their ears in waves they must ease
The Greeks know their stuff about how laws of sound
Can be used to harmonize wild loud underground.

Submariner Oisín knows oul Poseidon
He's seen him at work   knows where he's hidin'
How Hephaestos gets roilin   all rockin and rollin
And blasts all before him beyond all controllin
He knows all these G forces found deep in the earth
Must needs become known and given wide berth
They need their release   though loud they may be
The sound of their voices is pure minstrelsy
Though them who condemn it as voice of the divil
See evil at work and brand it uncivil.

IIII

But oul druid Cadhan could see how it might
Be the right sound for some to hear the odd night
So from hazel root sap he brews up a Coll
With an underground flavoured powerful ceol
That draws in the crowd from up Eagle's Rock
With Mojo like Fury to The Cross they will flock
And Zealous young bucks with blood in their eyes
Building Pictures with lovers till dawn's early rise
Jumpin Orbit and dancin right under The Screen
In a subterranean sonic shebeen.

So down in the earth the goin" is rough
To ride on its quakes you have to be tough
When small massive wave strikes   you go with the flow
Or your banjaxed and busted by wild undertow
Time runs amok in this vortex of sound
Freein oul druids from deep underground
One Rudhraic the Master of distillin thyme
And druid   MacSeain   pioneer in his prime
Of fillin the space between a man's ears
With sights neither given to tears nor to fears.

It's here the music that rings round the hills
And into this cavern so loudly spills
Pretty Child Backfire blows from the height
Of Craig na Shoke's Echo rocks of delight
The same Undertones of deep Serpent Sound
MeFisto brings Fury down low underground
To let out the Clutch of Tide's high Elation
Hy Brasil descendin to low elevation
A seismic shape shiftin tsunami scene
Rolls under The Cross and shakes up The Screen

Hell hath no Fury like this underworld
Where Angel Fall Coda Free Riders swirled
Where even our heroes are pushed to the brink
And need to ascend for a paeceable drink
But here neath Caith Oir there's always a place
For those in need of a quieter pace
And Fionn knows a druid just paces away
From a long line of folk   the Clan MacAmhalghaidh
In a tidy wee spot where paece is revered
And riotous noise will never be heerd.

The muse who inhabits this warm easy spot
Is the one for the crack who talks a wilelot
She hovers around personified here
As druidess Deirdre of the well tuned ear
She hears oul foolosophers solvin world's ills
And pours just enough from the bubblin stills
To keep the oul sophistry simmerin slow
Without boilin over and spoilin the flow
For here are some Ceallachs   Brollaghans too
MacUiginns also who have taken a few.

IIII

With whistles well wet the eloquence soars
But Deirdre knows it can all end in roars
If excess of spirits so loosens the tongue
That sconchin can scunner and laeve a boy stung
So Da Barnidh stills a toddy 'Oubh Coll
As his father before him delivered to all
To haet a coul harth to warm heart's desire
If the crack's goin' slack and dampens the fire
To the Greek argonauts from warm sunny clime
It's a cosy reminder of their own summertime.

All laed back and mellow our heroes decide
That maybe it's time their horse race to ride
But before they get mounted they hear a new sound
Yet another distraction to keep them around
For there by the Burnside music so sweet
Has them steppin out lightly on very big feet
'It's a MacCuin session'   says Fionn to his mates
'The druidess Faollain tonight celebrates.'
Cú Chulainn so eager for fiddledeedee
Leps across like a lilty as light as can be.

The sight of Cú Chulainn doin' his sevens
Is one for the ages under the heavens
The sight of the warrior up on his toes
Prancin through Burnside stealin the shows
Might make you think that Ciaragain taught him
For there was himself as if death never caught him
Cloggin Cú Chulainn just up Cath Oir Hill
The two of them tappin   you might hear them still
There's nothin like dancin to burn aff the steam
Preventin it ventin in combat extreme.

The Hound long in thrall to the The Morrigan caw
Now hears the call of the Ciaragan fleadh
The Master of War has succumbed to the trance
Givin in to wan foe   The Lord of the Dance
The pace of a man who knows what is right
Knowin body and space are tight   tight   tight
We're not as distinct as we think we are
So dance with that feelin and don't wage war
Instead of the clashin and slashin of swords
We're timin' the space by steppin the boards.

Now the women of Screen begin to come out
To see what the ruckus and racket's about
And soon they are joinin this rowdy sean nós
As Cú Chulainn jigs lively   back to The Cross
Where hornpipes struck up get danced to the beat
Of a band of Burnsiders with flame in their feet
A Muirgheas   a Seosamh   a Seamus in synch
A Brollaghan Cadhan Diamin rince
A pluckin   a thumpin   a scrapin and scourin
Steppin it out with bán bow and bodhran.

The Burnside is burnin this hot sweaty night
With ceol ceilidhe cailíní closin in tight
There's a wild bit of squeezin   squshin and squaelin
With hands findin places they love to be staelin
When out of the dark comes The Boss with a torch
To shine up the scene and see some skin scorch
'I can't sleep the night with this decadent dance.'
Shouts The Boss in a fit and ruins the trance
'It's you four again   get to Hell out of here.'
And sticks his big torch up Cú Chulainn's rear.

ᚷáe bolga   ᚷáe bolga' is Cú Chulainn's cry
'If I had you now this blackrobe would die.'
But he cools it again with heroic restraint
If he wasn't heathen he might be a saint
Pullin the torch from his still smokin bum
He looks at The Boss and gives him the thumb
'Be GAA Zeus' he says *'I needed that now*
The grapes are a bugger ye know anyhow
You're a dab han at that   practice   I'm sure
Burnin in Burnside's a wonderful cure.'

But worse is to come when the heroes decide
That dark is the time their horses to ride
They saddle up smartly   get set and go
Top speed through the burn by silver moon glow
Hoof smoke and sparks light up the Burnside
Tonagh Hill falls behind   their steeds in full stride
Through woods and through meadows   ditches and shughs
There's joy in the ride of these tipsy young bucks
With Cú Chulainn ahead by Salann box lane
Oghma in second grippin Pegasus mane.

7. Stragh Dog Straes

Down Mala MacRahallaigh's deep into Straw
Where they see a Stragh dog astray of the law
Come runnin out boldly to snap at the hooves
Of any horse power near Sean Mullagh moves
Cú Chulainn just laughs at the stray dog attack
But not Liath Macha who takes a stride back
Rears up and kicks down at this fearless wee dog
Near buckin Cú Chulainn up into the bog
Says he   'Yer a game one   ye mongrel pup.'
Reachin down till he scoops it   draggin it up.

The dog digs his teeth in Cú Chulainn's hand
As if to say   'Get the hell off my land
We don't want ye here   just rallyin roun
Especially not you   ye bloodsuckin houn.'
Just one week ago our hero might just
Have swallied this pup as dogs of war must
But then he remembers the Morrigan's geis
And how Screen Spirit is changin his ways
So he sets the dog down   sayin 'We'll meet again
....

The manuscript here is badly burnt. We don't know what else might have been said to the dog or whether more verses were lost. One fragment of burnt vellum has the words "dog slain by Mercmobille   Cluain" but we don't know whether it is the same dog described above.

The race resumes ...

Not far behind   it's Oisín on Dollaigh
Fionn at the back on a slowin down Darcaigh
Until by the river his race is in muck
And Dollaigh bucks Oisín into a shugh
When she sees the Whitewater she's had enough
Somethin beyond it spookin her rough
They've been here before and feel dread ahead
They won't lead nor drive   no farther will tread
With eyes that are wile and mouths full of foam
They turn back and stand near their own stable home.

The Owl Boy's stable's a warm place to stap
For horses and men to take a wee drap
Of life givin uisce aether well or from still
It's a comfort to all who grind at the mill
Says Fionn *'We're lossin the race but what odds*
I'm sure them horses must think we are cods
Gallivantin about in the dead of night
Hell bent in a race to win bummin right
Let thon two go on if hell they do reach
Then hell rub it up them it's haet that'll teach.'

Cú Chulainn and Oghma are fordin Whitewater
Unbeknownst to their mounts it's Díseart dark matter
Now speedin for Shibbigh's pell mell to hell
The hill crooked cross starts casting its spell
When they catch sight of the black Díseart cross
Both horses are trimmlin ready to toss
At Shibbigh's they come to a hoof grindin halt
The horses refusin to lead drive or vault
Past the spectres that haunt this ill crossed place
Where manys a chariot ended its chase.

The words of Cú Chulainn about not reachin hell
Have come back to haunt him painfully well
While Oghma himself thinks this Underworld gate
Is as far as he'll go at any fast rate
When the spirits all broken   filled with remorse
Come gory and waelin up close to his horse
Pegasus throws him and boults for the stars
Has enough of this race and graveyard of cars
And Liath Macha too   spooked by the ghouls
Thinks drinkin and ridin is only for fools.

He bucks off Cú Chulainn right into the ditch
And speeds for the hills like he's hit by a switch
While two mighty champions now stranded there
Forlornly mount up on lowly shank's mare
Accompanied by ghosts of carnage and famine
They are loathe to engage or closely examine
Half runnin towards Stragh through Whitewater foam
To find at The Owl Boy's a haven like home
Where the druid prepares to stiffen their spines
With a Straif served straight   one of Stragh's moonshines.

####

In the realms of spirits Stragh is unmatched
It's here that the dark side is deeply dispatched
With the stout juice of blackthorn used in defence
The ghosts of the past can't marshal offense
Agin porter's barbarous bitter black bLas
They fade claen away and through the night pass
Cú Chulainn and Oghma back from the dead
Toast the sons of The Owl Boy out in their shed
That's fillin up now with local hard men
Avoidin the forces with whom they contend.

Dom Buideal is there and An Guil Lir comes in
And sharp-witted hAodh ~ again whose sconchin can skin
An Nabhaigh an hEarain and the two brothers Maolain
All enter the stable and nod to Cú Chulainn
An Doch   a Tomhrar and some Ceallach tribes
Like the slow talkin Tríona who never imbibes
A Coscrachan choirster who sang of his ma
And An Bing who'd recite a verse about Stragh
Rhymed tight by a Cianan who missed his oul home
From which many like him were once forced to roam.

Cú Chulainn and Fionn both say in accord
'Ye can't let them Skinners over ye lord
What yous want's a Fianna that stands up and fights
A league of the land of oak branch knights
Sconchin the Skinners who've skint yous alive
Not fightin with fists but fly to their skive
The boys in the stable   a wile bunch we know
But they know the schaeme   why Skinners ye owe
That Ogle wee ogre ye owe's but a pup
These boys'll get ye top doG if yous only wise up.

Yous have to unite like the Wolf in a pack
Tone down the whingin and whinin sad sack
Ye must howl together howlin in time
To draw in the Law and the doGmaster prime
The Bulldog Himself who thinks he can fight
A Barker whose Bark's far worse than His Bite
It's Him yous are after   the doG in yer head
No pike or pitchfork will puncture Him dead
But a pome pair verse can reverse the doG
It's up to the Owl Boy to give us first jog.'

There in the corner   his cap on his knob
The Owl Boy himself   his pipe in his gob
Says he to Cú Chulainn *'What is the news?*
Yer horses arrived with nether of yous
If ye can't howl the horses   keep them in rein
How will ye give me stables a claen?
Me sons are unstable can't get them to graep
Yous look no better at claenin thon haep.'
'Don't worry'   says Oghma   *'we'll claen the place*
There's more than wan way to run a good race.'

The scene it is set for a night worth a lay
Muse news on the wing across Comhrac Uae
Rooks roostin on headstones in clearest moonshine
Cawin   versin   crow cryptin on Cross humankind
'Auk naw' croaks The Raven   *'It's caws in me grief*
This carrion here caws in ᚷıoᒪᒪᗪ and chief
To be unearthed and moved caws Mercmobille horde
Must carry waens fast caws The Boss can't afford
To loss any time caws so dearly bought
These crypt robbin rooks must gravely be taught.'

####

Such caws have effects on spirits who've passed
Right through the holes the worms have cast
Their faint floatin forms flow through the gable
Past druid shades who've been in this stable
Mac Eoghain and Uí Néill dispensin the ᴅeoch
The Owl Boy an' Maolain keepin Stragh Straif in stock
The Brollaghan boys   SeoCrig and SeanSeo
Then Dherigh then Seosamh then Peadar go
Together distillin the spirit of Straw
Keepin punters sup plied and an eye on The Law.

The singin and versin's about to begin
When who but Dhim Dhiabhal comes urgently in
Says he   *'I'm roastin for want of a tot*
The work down thonder's infernally hot
This burnin the damned works up a wile druth
It's a hell of a job tae tell ye the truth'
'So why don't ye quet?'   says Cú Chulainn to him
'Ye don't know Yer Man'   says drinched in sweat Dhim
'This job is foriver there's no end in sight
It's enough to make ye want t'be eternally tight.'

Then into the stable comes Brollaghan Seo
'Keep it down boys'   says Seo   *'The Law's on the go*
Yer Man has his rules no singin the night
Past closin time now   keep yer gobs closed tight.'
The stable goes dead   not a rhyme is heard
But the Coscrachan boy' not aesy scared
'Maa maa mee' he sings   arms out   on his knee
The minstrel in him would not let it be
So the stable goes bedlam and Seo's back again
'Will yis wheest or Dog Daddy will cause us great pain.'

The stable goes quaet   a wile silent night
Not a hymn not a hum not a hiss so slight
But silence was fraught with a tension taut
Like the strings of a harp so wantin caught
By a hiccup   belch or a lettin off
An Bing to the rescue   whisperin soft
Begins to recite from Cianan's oul verse
But instead of relief makes the tension worse
For the ode from afar to times long ago
Makes them keenin Strawdogs in howls high and low.

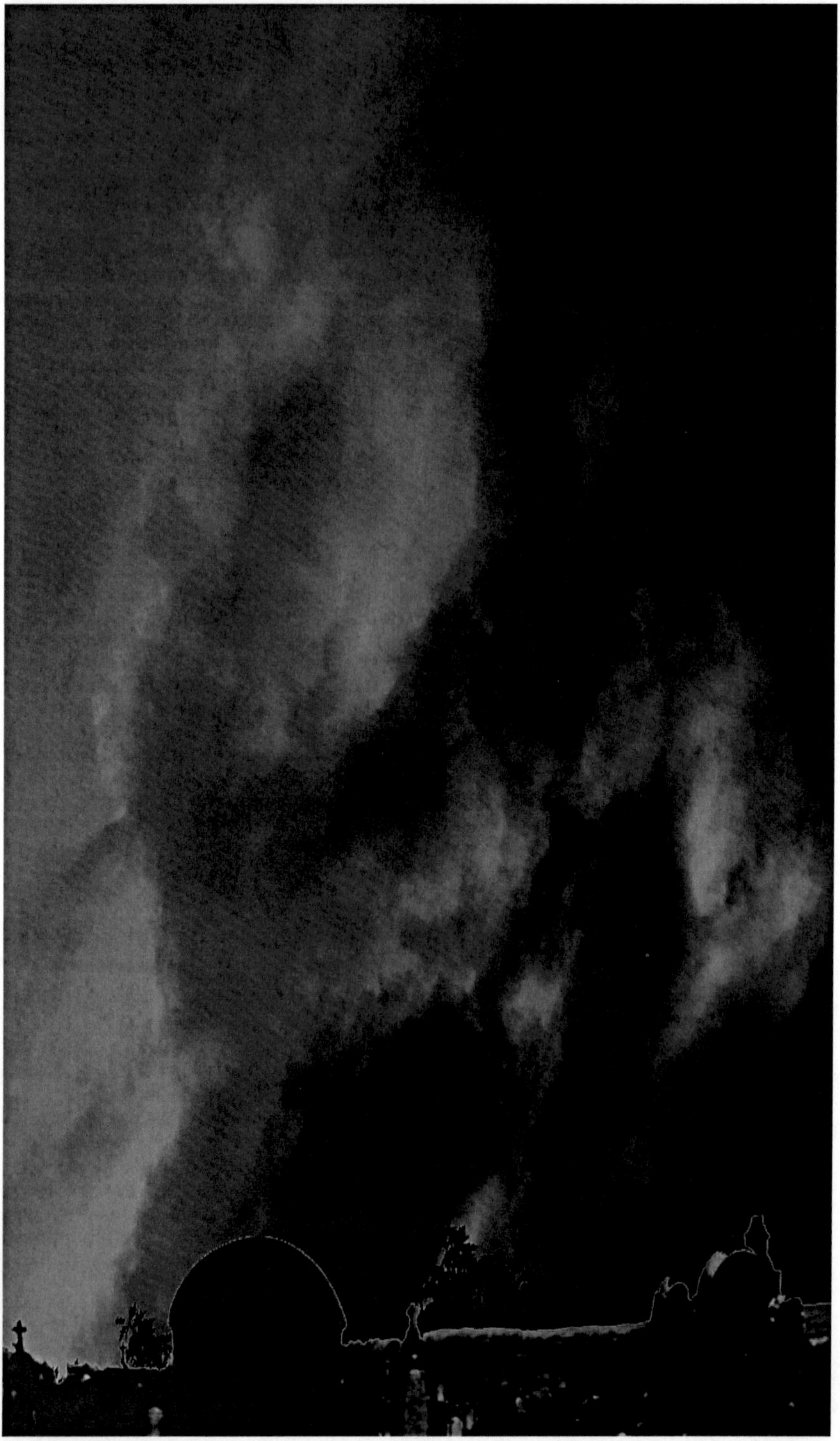

Such loud lamentations draws in The Law
Not just Ola Mór or The Boss's the draw
But Yer Man doG Da   All Mighty All Awe
GAAZeus? Oh God Aye   God Oh   right in Straw
A massive big ganch   a Cnoc Mór with feet
Who bulls His way in to that stable retreat
He wields a big club   a thick camán rod
And drags round behind   His tremendhous bod
About His coorse head   a cláirseach of oak
With hundreds of strings though most of them broke.

In all of his days in battles galore
Cú Chulainn has seen the wilest Fir Mór
But never a ganch with the girth like thon
'This boy'll crush me if I take him on
Me slither of ash wull split like a match
Me sword or me spear wull not laeve a scratch.
Me Gáe Bolga wouldn't   make even a dent
This calls for some sconchers of sharp temperament'
So he winks at an hAodh ~ again and nods at the bod
Says he *'Would ye jist take a luck at the taus on thon cod.'*

Yer Man doesn't bite   makes nary a sound
But searches the face of each sittin round
The stable goes dark but they can just spy
By glint of moonglow   He's got but one eye
He plucks His oak harp   the longest thick whang
That makes them near deef with ear drummin twang
Then hoists His big bod above His head height
And swings it around with lambeggin might
In a dirty black blur   a bull roarin blare
Beginnin to drag   in all of them there.

A vortex of black   Yer Man's eye at its heart
The great spinnin bod could rip Straw apart
And turn it to chaff in the blink of His eye
But just stoppin short at the brink lettin fly
The tipplers can feel it suckin them in
The heads fair liftin in thunderous din
Big bubbles of snot spewin out of its core
All that is left of its swallied gore
Then He whaels it straight down   an Almighty Pound
Till the stable fluer quaeks deep under the ground.

From his gigantic gob a great gulder roars
Through spit   snot and slabber   this tirade he pours
*'Are you seein Me now   make Meself clear?
Do I have to be special   can all of yous hear?
IT'S CLOSIN TIME NOW   YOUR TIME HERE IS UP'*
And he turns to Dhim Diabhal who's taekin a sup
*'Get up off your hole and back down below
There's work to be done where these boys'll go
Now shift it   get goin"   judgement day's here
These goats in this stable must suffer severe.'*

'Ach howl on a bit sure what is the rush?'
Says Cú Chulainn   givin luck a big push
'Sit a wee while   take the load aff yer back
Sure how is she cuttin   how is the crack?'
Yer Man flails around in a lather of spit
His bod raised aloft   Cú Chulainn to hit
'NONE OF YOUR LIP'   says Yer Man very loud
I've heard about you   too cute and too proud.'
'I tell ye what boy'   says Fionn to Yer Man
'That's wan mighty bod   how high can it stan?'

An Tríona chips in   a staid sober judge
'A tune on your harp   please do not begrudge.'
Before He has time to take in the crack
An hAodh ~ again chimes in with a different tack
'Ach play us a kune on that lovely harp
The singin here's flat   sure You'll keep us sharp'
'And I'll sing Tútsigh'   says Coscrachan too
'If you tune her up I'll be croonin for you'
'Aye'   says An Guile Lir   'I'll get Ye Stragh Tae
Aw aye a uisce   it'll help Ye tae play.'

85

Lard tunderin GAAZeus Yer Man has a fit
'ENOUGH OF THIS CRACK   I don't drink or sit
This cláirseach stays mute   you'll not hear it play
Till you're all in hell on this Judgment Day.'
Yer Man will not budge   will not lead nor drive
It's lookin wile black but who should arrive
But Cormac Na Cláirseach   timeshifter of Dún
Says he   *'Did I hear a big string so far out of tune?*
It brattled the air away cross the Screen?
Says I   *'This is wan harp that has to be seen.'*

'Cormac   come in'   says Fionn from the dark
We have a boy here with a cuirc in his cuarc
Won't play us a tune on his charmin harp
He's lept on us hard   up and down sharp
Collidin with all and spoilin the crack.'
'That is a concern'   says timewright Cormac
'I have this wee notion that vibratin strings
Are what make us think we're seein things
This boy and his harp are very high strung
I'd hate to harp on it but his din is dung.'

'This matter is dark   this midden is muck
It takes away lenth and breath in its suck
A stable black hole that won't soon decay
The waves of that reek need washin away.'
Yer Man has a spasm   Cú Chulainn would say
As mad as his own on Táin battle day
The once stable stable unstable becomes
The dubh of the duhill the air vacuums
So bad is the reek   the rook runs awry
With no rhyme or reason the musin' will die.

'Is there anyone here'   says Cormac to all
'Knows how to claen such a dubh chokin pall?'
'Me sons are unstable'   The Owl Boy admits
'They're gone in a flash they have me in fits
They don't want to claen this haep a manure
There's pee on the groun   Cac na Bhó's on the fluer.'
But Oghma responds   *'I know the dubh poll*
I've seen it before   thon Ódhian hole
When my life was hell as some of yous know
The only way out   twelve jobs on the go'

86

'And the dirtiest   darkest   deed needin done
Is the grim grimy graft of graepin the dung
The only solution is sluicin the slime
With a race from the river rushin in time
It be to be true like an arra let fly
Right through His brain   split beam in His eye
I'm hopin' you   Tríona   in particle you'll are
Will help keep our eyes on Straw Mountain far.'
'Count on me   Cormac'   says Tríona   'All set
For one cold shootout   Straw won't soon forget'

An Bing who's been quaet since his Cianan rhyme
Is now comin out with own lines in chime
'There's no better river to sluice Cac na Bhó
Cac Dubh cannot thole thon Whitewater flow
It's run be me home since I was a waen
Floods flushin the filth agaen and agaen
We're expectin hard rain to give flood a heft
But who'll run the race in the time we've left?'
'No trouble at all'   says An Nabhaigh at wance
'I'll run the race   jist give me the chance.'

But all of this sconchin is not gettin through
Yer Man needs distractin as men often do
By a vision of beauty   a womanly form
When into the stable comes the perfect storm
'O Where is my lover   where is my man?'
Says the sweetest of voices soft as she can
In that desperate darkness dimly perceived
Her fragrant dark form just barely believed
By the drinkers   Yer Man   the cuddy and bó
All of them speechless at this dream now on show.

Only Cú Chulainn knows he's no dreamer
She's lookin for him   this is his Eimear
Seven suns in the Screen she has let him roam
He's crawled long enough   she's wantin him home
But before he can howl a howl of delight
He sees in the dark a deep pressin sight
Yer Man's single eye all red with blood shot
Is glaerin at Eimear and lookin besot
He feels somethin move   rise up off the fleur
And hears Yer Man groan at Eimear's allure.

Yer Man's bod is climbin   stiff and erect
Till it glows in the dark to awful effect
But risin so quick it really lets fly
The head of it hits Him right in the eye
While all in the stable see it's their chance
To run for their lives as He does a pain dance
And gropes in a frenzy   blind as a bat
Cú Chulainn steers Eimear where safety's at
Yer Man throws his harp but misses them all
It ends up at Míls's   a resoundin fall.

Where Cormac redeems it starts in to string
Soon gets it to hum and soundly to ring
While An Nabhaigh directs the rest of the crew
To dig a deep ditch right all the way through
From Comhrac to Straw in no time at all
Through duhill and stable through every stall
Where Yer Man still stummlin   howlin in pain
His hard on collidin His eye with His brain
Till He hears His own harp strung out over Straw
And clouds rumblin down from a skyful of awe.

Cormac gets pluckin the highest wee strings
A breeze comin up and spittin rain brings
He moves down the strings so oak starts to brattle
Goin' in deeper like Táin Titan battle
The wined shakes the Screen to make it vibrate
With a base boomin thump slammin weight
Cormac na Fisic strikes string sparkin bolts
'GAAZeus'   says Oghma   '*jist look at them jolts*
Great Atlas himself could hardly howl thon.'
'*Aye*'   says an hAodh ~ again   '*Yer Man'll be gone.*'

Split by fork lightnin in blue ragged rays
Black clouds collidin over Sliabh Gallon Braes
Straw Mountain   Comhrac and Breachach explode
In water spout falls unleashin their load
As Black and Whitewater rush to the race
A tempest wave high at a Pegasus pace
Swallys the stable   Him blinded within
Yer Man and manure in a whirlpool spin
A flurry of slurry in spiral full bore
Flush down the dam hole in deepest Strawmore.

IIII

'Good riddance'   says Fionn   'I thought we were toast
All that crack about hell and how we would roast
Has me feelin the druth for a Seosaimh Stragh Sail
That he turns from racewater to blackest Sail ale.'
'Take yer pick '   Seosaimh says   'pick wan of three
Sail on   sail on   sail on race dam or sea
We'll toast our escape from Yer Man's big bod
So here's to the heroes who baet The Oul Sod
Here's to the woman who started the fray
The mammy come lookin for daddy at play.'

'There's a war on ye know '   Eimear now says
'While you're in the Screen still suppin its taes
That Medb woman's marchin on our Uladh soil
I thought ye were wounded by Táin battle toil
You're lookin bravely   I see no scars here.'
Says Cú Chulainn   'Screen spirits make scars disappear
They soothe and they heal all slashes and cuts
Glue on severed bits   close holes in the guts
When I arrived here life hung by a string
If not for Screen spirit I'd be missin me thing.'

'Aye   right'   Eimear says   'It's time ye were home
The waens need their da but you drink and roam
Get out of the Screen   it'll do yer head in
Get back on the job reddin and beddin
Or it's closin time boy   it's over   it's done
Enough gallivantin   you've had yer fun.'
'Ach now Eimear   ye sound like Yer Man
Just wan more night in the Screen   just wan
There's a ceili the night   right here in Straw
At the Banba they tell me does the crowds draw.'

The thought of a dance makes Eimear's head light
'We could do with a jig   I suppose it's all right'
She gives him the eye he's longin to see
And slips an arm round him   so nice and free
Says he   'Let's go me darlin   it's already on
We'll dance through the night till Straw's early dawn'
The head for the Banba   arm in arm now
Followed by tipplers from thon stable row
And the music's soon heard just up Comhraic Uae
That sets them up steppin a Banba display.

91

The Banba is jumpin with jiggers in pairs
Disportin   cavortin to jigs   reels and airs
By a band a musicians from all round the Screen
hEgartaigh   Maolain and Ceallachs a wheen
Wan Ceallach sαoR αᴅhmαιᴅ   fast fiddlin fine
Has the weemen of Screen step swingin divine
This Bhachadh   like Tríona   does not imbibe
But gets drunk on the lilt of his musical tribe
Cuttin time   rollin time   bouncin his bow
Tellin time by horse tale and ridin' the flow.

The music goes slippin and slidin in time
So the past and the future be present in rhyme
The band of the Banba is joined in their play
By the likes of a Muireadh and Mac Ainmhire
From times fore and aft beyond the green Screen
From townlands afar in the Gleann of Con Cadhain
Mac Uistin   Coill   and Mac Giolla Buidhe
Hornpipin   slide jiggin   stomp swingin free
To a time when the dancin is done in a ring
Where right and left hooks and uppercuts swing.

Just when you think the clamjamphrie's done
The Banba herself drops in for the fun
The stage it is set   the Sparks start to fly
The Woman in White is luckin a lie
The drama is high   not mellow or sad
She dances with hAodh ~ again spinnin him mad
Then with An Doc   An Guil Lir   An Bing
Grabs anyone roun and gives them a fling
Till none of them knows their off from their on
Their now from the then   their this from their thon.

There's a change of tune under Banba's moon
Her dance demandin a time
That's tricky to baet   too early or late
And the steps won't join up or chime
So who should come in but a boy from Cloch Fhionn
A Brolaigh to squeeze out the notes
His stoppin is poppin   the Banba is hoppin
A chord he's on rises and floats
To a Truailleain Dubh who gets squeezin too
As he tickles the reeds till they sing
And nobody sits but gets up and flits
For the Banba to give them a swing.

She tries every man not playin the band
Not one of them fit for her spin
Till she catches sight of Cú Chulainn in flight
With Eimear reelin him in
She calls on the band with a key command
And they follow her biddin and swing
When she gives the sign   the Ceallach's in line
His horsehair scrapin the string
She makes a pair three   one he and two she
With Cú Chulainn and Eimear in hand
The woods sweetly hum to the just heard drum
Of Brolaigh foot tappin the band.

The Ceallach he's sayin *'This music we're playin*
Is The Tune The Oul Cow Died With
The Mad Cow of Craobh   we Strawmen believe
It Danced Claen Out of its Hide With.'
The Banba says *'Wheest   jist play Ballybriest*
That tune's From Cow Lough To Boolia
Jist Lissan and go with The Blackwater Flow
Don't let Thon Breacach Bull fool ye.'
So he takes her advice   starts playin it nice
And easy at first   then faster
As Whitewater Falls   he fiddles and stalls
But Runs In The Race nearly past her.

She skips a Cross Reel   and kicks up her heel
She's High Cauld Cappin it fast
Tory Waves lashin   Limerick Walls crashin
Ennis Siege liftin at last
Banba goes local   un equi vocal
Her music is rooted in Screen
It Trips on a Stragh to Fall in Dún Fleadh
Glen Gamhna Jigs on The Green
They go Comhraic O   She Step Tonagh Toe
He does the Shibigh Sleigh Slide
Down Díseart he Dips   to Kiss Labby Lips
She does a Bancran Glibe Glide.

Banba does sevens   up Sliabh Gallon heavens
Cú Chulainn keeps fallin right back
Her tunes are all new   to his quick wife too
But Eimear is gettin the knack
Quick Step to Cahore   High step to Cnoc Mór
Back step to Strawmore or Less
Stap a Spell on Spelhoagh   on Dunlogan Shelf
With Mad Moneyneena don't mess
Lep steps to The Rock Where Young Eagles Flock
Moss Mosh to Moydamlaght Muse
Don't skip or avoid   Do Dance Derrynoid
Or sing The Ballynure Blues.

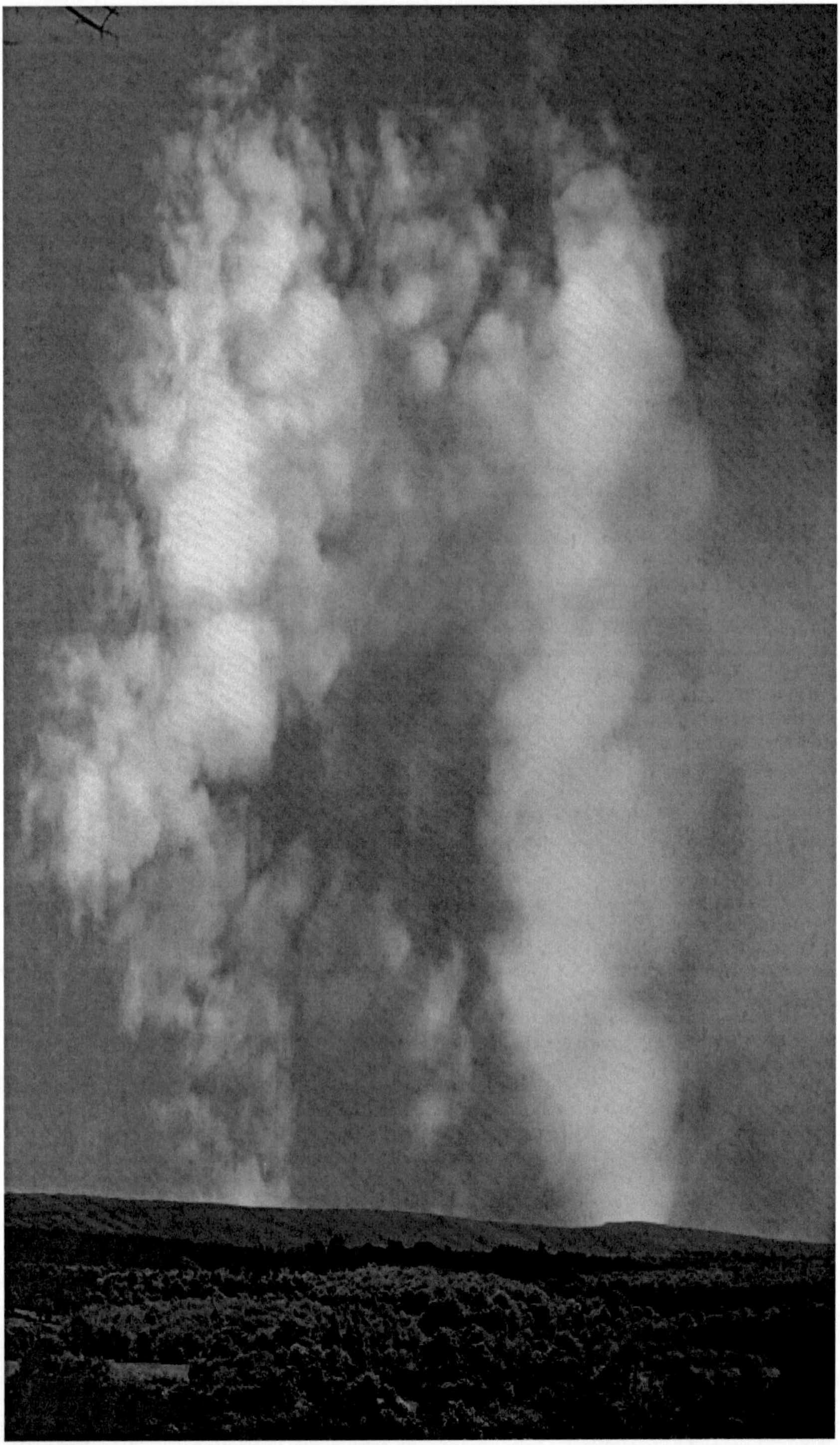

Cú Chulainn has strenth   but two arms the wan lenth
Means he can't bate Drumderg alone
But gets a tip there   how to Drumard the Dair
And Mulnavoo Ewe into Cluain
If he's Dún Muiri Dance   there's Carnamoney Chance
He'll keep Coolnasillagh In Sight
He's gettin the hang   of This Glebe Shebang
His Moneyquiggy Jig nice n tight
Three notes in a chord   Two Ladies and Lord
They move through Moykeeran In Style
No Duntibryan Dunt   no Gortnaskey Grunt
They skite up The Straight Five Mile.

In a Screen wide swing   Under Banba's Wing
They land be a Steep Owenreagh
Where Tullybrick Hard   touches Sweet Moyard
In the shade of a Crockbrack Brae
Moneyconey rhyme   Glenviggan in time
Last steps to The County March
And that's when they go a quick step too slow
For their rhythm lost they must sarch
When a nudged elbow or a stood on toe
By a sly MacThreinfir not playin
But jist for the crack when the goin's slack
Sends Brolaigh's fingers astrayin.

Brolaigh's wild mad at this traetment bad
But his ire inspires a tune
A tune from the past when the Banba cast
Her spell by the light of the moon
At a crossroads dance where a rough romance
In the Doire Not Far Away
Was a threesome rare Atap Roots of Dair
When lovers glimpsed stars at play
Past wee oak spring leaves where the night sky heaves
With gods glowin over Cnoc Mór
In a Milky Way putting heads astray
With love never felt before.

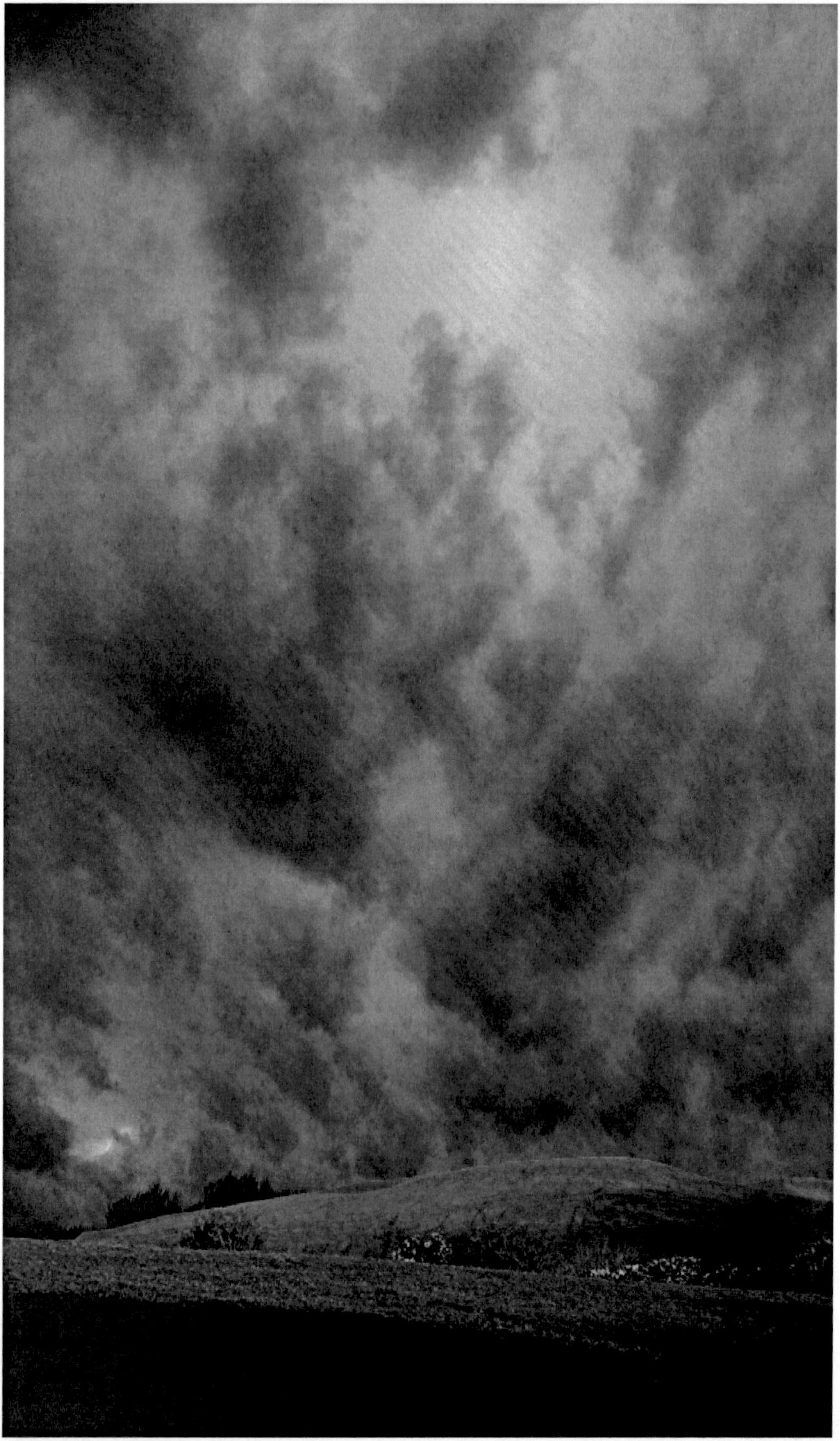

A chord he intones that the Banba owns
Her secret one felt in the bones
So the dancers halt for a beat or two
While the band makes an oul time new
But Cú Chulainn trips   on a reel he slips
As his feet footer flat till he flips
But the Banba's beat gets his two left feet
On a footin fleet where the trio meet
At ᚐon ᚑó ᚈrí ceaᚈhair cúiᚌ sé seaᚉhᚈ
With a knees up naoi ᚑeich cúirᚈéireaᚉhᚈ.

'Cú Chulainn'   says Eimear   'who taught you to ʀınce?'
'Screen spirit'   says he   'is not all about drink
But lets you feel time's a to and fro foe
Where its future's behind   its past is on show
Out there   straight ahead   in space   past is seen
Its future's back there behind the Screen scene
If you go roun the Screen   keepin always afoot
Drink in each townland   time's arrow'll shoot
Right back where it curved   you're feelin it dance
Screen spirit sees past it   through it   in trance.

'Yer talkin oul guff'   says Eimear and smiles
As she dances the Banba right down to Míls
Where the woodlands of Stragh ruled by the Dair
Form a doire that runs to the mill from there
With the new race a racin'   turnin a wheel
So Ceallach the miller   its power can steal
Servin time   savin time   grindin time down
Before its fermented   distilled   seen aroun
To a future that's dark when Straw's in the town
Space and time curvin   to a string hummin soun.

There in the doire   Cú Chulainn goes mad
With laughin delight at the fortune he's had
To be with this woman right here in the grove
For the last time   he knew   so he strove
To lap every vale of her silken skin
Moanin an groanin with joy goin' in
Her cries ringin out way over the Screen
Their branches entwined   their limbs in between
The leaves of their lovin whisper and tease
Their doire airs bare a dair in the breeze.

The Banba in Eimear beneath seven vales
Where silver Screen waters flow down her dales
Sailin Moyola upstream to her source
Explorin the brooks that swell her great course
Where bright Altalacky and Dunlogan Burn
Where Drumderg and Glasagh clear waters churn
Where Glen Gomhna waters glitter and gleam
Where Moyola herself is just a wee stream
Up the Whitewater where Banba turns Black
Slips swift Altagoan down Sliabh Gallon's back
Banba through Eimear   Cú Chulainn in flight
All come in a flood of ecstatic delight.

As they languish and laze in the lap of the oak
The Raven swoops down with a Stragh dark croak
It lands on Cú Chulainn and gives him a wink
'It's closin time soon' croaks The Raven *'I think'*
'I know' says Cú Chulainn *'it's there in yer eye*
The future behind reflectin me die
I'm ready an willin to croak without fear
No kneelin to gods that aren't near and dear
No squakin for mercy in face of dark wrath
When I hear yer last call I'll folly yer path.'

'I want to be battlin on me feet free
And when I'm too waek go find a Dair tree
To tie meself up to its mighty trunk
No kneelin for me but want to go drunk
The Dair of Screen spirit just proppin me up
Dair tree for the frame Dair drink the mind's sup.'
Winkin back at the corbie who cuarcs *'Fair enough*
I'll be seein you there but the end'll be rough
I'll be aetin yer eyes out wance you've croaked.'
Says Cú Chulainn *'You're welcome to them I'll keep them well soaked.'*

These Morrigan words exchanged in regard
The time for farewells now would be hard
It's back to oul Míls for a partin poitín
With Oghma   hAodh ~ again   Fionn   Doch and Oisín
Maolain   Dhim Diabhal   Coscrachan   Bing
Cormac   the Owl Boy   An Nabhaigh   all sing
Druid Dhim Micí Eoghain sup lyin Dair pot
That even frank Bhachadh and Tríona take tot
All raisin a jar to a battle well fought
Turnin time's arrow before they be caught.

Back down Bothar Buí to the Táin they go
Cú Chulainn and Eimear takin it slow
A kiss every townland they cross in between
The Plain of Muirtheimne and Baile na Scrín
Prepared for the worst   full facin his fate
In defence of the land and his lovely mate
While back in the Screen with time standin still
Awaitin the spirit to full the glass fill
Last sound ringin out from the Whitewater vale
Is the keenin Strawdogs as they howl and wail.

We turn now from doggerel crawl and drunken brawl back to the "real" history of the drink in Ballinascreen.

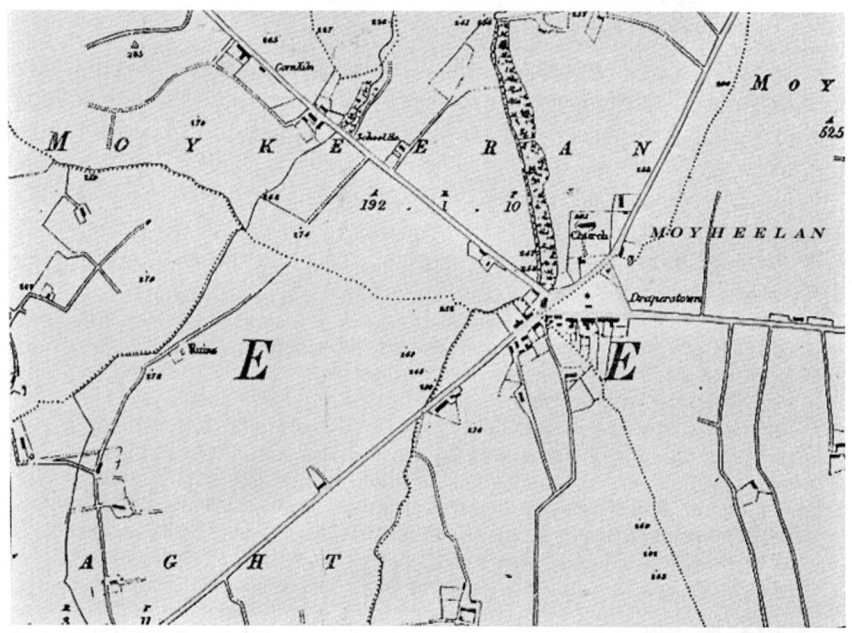

Below; **An Bothar Buí** in 1827. Why was Draperstown first called "The Yellow Road"? Did it refer to that spiritual journey as in the Yellow-brick road to Emerald City or the road to **Fleð Goibniu**-inspired enlightenment in **Tír na nÓg** or the colour added to poitín to make it look like Parliament Whiskey or was it because of the great numbers of livestock and drinkers, half-tore and hefted, on the road on Fair Days? All of the above?

An Bothar Buí

("Borbury" - the yellow road)
"a comfortable place to take his glass in"

1798 was an eventful year in Ireland. Wolfe Tone and the boys were rebelling and the great town of An Bothar Buí was being born. The founder of this embryonic Draperstown was, not an architect, a town planner or a politician but maybe aptly enough, given later developments, a publican, one Laughlin McNamee, in circumstances that look familiar when cattle dealers get together for a drink ... in a tent.

Here is how it all came about according to the *Ordnance Survey Memoirs for the Parish of Ballynascreen of 1836* ;

> "Before 1797 the cattle fair had always been held in the townland of Moneyneany. In that year, at one of the fairs, the company in McNamee's tent became quarrelsome over their liquor. Their ideas suddenly received a new turn by one of the drunkards exclaiming that if he had a house at one of the crossroads he would "have a comfortable place to take his glass in," upon which, after some further altercation, another rushed out, and leaping on a cart, proclaimed to the multitudes that the next fair would be held at the crossroads of Moyheyland. They accordingly resorted thither at the time appointed and immediately Laughlin McNamee removed to it and built the first houses. He also established a weekly market by giving free cranage and entertainment, and to this day it, as well as the principal part of the fair, is held **about his doorway**.
>
> With the priest's aid at first, and then the gentry, he kept down quarrelling, and soon had the satisfaction of seeing the fair in a flourishing state and the number of houses increasing. He named it first **Borbury** or the *"yellow road"* then **Moyheyland** then **Ballynascreen**, the **Cross**, then **Draperstown Cross** and finally **Draperstown**.

Was that tent in Moneyneena a "public house"? Were all drinking establishments at that time, temporary structures? We have to assume that McNamee built a more solid one at the Cross and it was probably an early precursor of the one that would become McNamee's Hotel that lasted into the 1970's? The one that is now **the shamrock**? This Laughlin McNamee seems to be the same gentleman mentioned in the McNamee-Regan-Kelly family tree, (McLaughlin=McNamee, a marriage) eight generations back from Dennis and Johnny McNamee who worked the bar and adjoining butcher shop near "the Cross" in my own young days. He is an ancestor of mine too, the great-great grandfather of Evlin Duffy who married my paternal great grandfather, Peter Kelly in the first half of the 1800's. Another branch of the McNamees was linked by marriage to the Regan line and that union led to a veritable dynasty of publicans (and butchers) in the Draperstown and Maghera areas, a dynasty which is still going strong with three pubs and a butcher's shop in the Regan name.

From the Ordnance Survey (1836), here is part of the entry for Trades and Occupations (with a rather disapproving sounding note about 'societies').

> Except the Draperstown branch of the North West Farming Society, *there are no societies for the encouragement of useful arts or inventions.*
> spirit sellers 6   blacksmith and spirit sellers 1
> grocers and spirit sellers 2   labourers 4   grocers 4
> shoemakers 3 wheelwright 1   carpenter 1... etc

Not only was the town founded by a publican but the main occupation of its inhabitants, nearly 40 years on, was *spirit selling!* 9 spirit sellers out of 39 individuals listed under various occupations! 23% of the "usefully" employed were selling liquor? Does this mean that the good people of Ballinascreen were very fond of the drink? Not at all. From the 1821 statistical report for Ballinascreen, Kilcronaghan and Desertmartin no such charge was made ...

> Notwithstanding the late surprising increase of illicit distillation, the *prodigious number of shebeen houses,* the facility for procuring spirits and the general use of them, *habitual intemperance is very rare*: and without intentional offense.

Poteen and Shebeen in the Screen

Maybe these parishes loved their shebeens and public houses simply because the people were sociable, not because they were inveterate drinkers. But in that 1821 report there is a reference to 142 distillers keeping accounts with the Desertmartin malt mill alone and it's likely that many of these distillers were to be found hard at work in the relatively remote mountainous areas of Ballinascreen where detection by the excise man was less likely than in the wide open spaces of Tobermore and Desertmartin where more law abiding "settlers" were in the majority. In the 1836 Survey we have this note; *"Illicit distillation is still carried on in the mountains and is usually concealed very ingeniously."* (not below?)

Gather up the pots and the old tin cans
The mash, the corn, the barley and the bran.
Run like the devil from the excise man.

The following stories are told by a Tyrone "Son of the Sperrins" who knew a certain poitín maker very well in a place close to Ballinascreen.

Spirit Forge

After the First World War, scarcity and poor quality of materials were problems for tradesmen. Taidg the Smith complained bitterly of the poor quality of iron and coal.

One cold wintry day, a neighbour passing the forge dropped in with a bottle of poitín. Taidg liked to drink and soon the bottle was well on the way to empty. As they were talking and sharing the bottle, two police officers on bicycles approached the forge and entered, to warm up, as they were very cold. Taidg, who held the bottle, turned quickly as they entered, shoved the cork back in, and buried the bottle in the ashes and cinders at the front of the hearth. The two officers, glad to get a chance to warm up, engaged in conversation with the two neighbours, who lost no opportunity to complain about bad times, bad British policy, and in the case of Taidg, bad British coal and iron.

In the course of the conversation, the bottle, heated as it was, suddenly exploded, sending ashes, cinder, and slack over the anvil and the group. Taidg, as quick-witted as he was handy, quickly explained,
"That bloody English coal is getting worse."

Fiery Spirit

Paddy C of Gortin was a veteran of the Irish War of Independence and a firm believer in the slogan, 'Ireland Sober is Ireland Free'. He hated and despised all forms of alcohol consumption.

One day in the 1920s, one of his farm labourers found a bottle of poitín hidden in a hedge on Paddy's farm. He gave it to Paddy, who took it home.

Paddy arranged to convey information on 'the find' to a couple of notorious local 'druths'. They were told that they would be welcome to visit him.

In due course, this was arranged, and the duo were glad to see that Paddy had displayed the bottle prominently on his kitchen table, significantly partnered with two empty whisky glasses.

After the usual neighbourly conversation, Paddy poured a glass and said, "I just heard that this stuff would burn." So he spilled a few drops on the open hearth, with a bright blue flame resulting. "Isn't that amazing." he said, adding a few drops, and a few more, until the glass was empty.
Another glassful was sacrificed to a continuation of the experiment, with Paddy repeating, "I never thought this stuff would burn!" and the two visitors becoming increasingly disconsolate and suspicious.

Eventually, after the fourth glass of poitín had been consigned to the fire, they politely took their leave and went their way, thoughtful and sober. Paddy triumphantly disposed of the bottle, glass by glass, in the fire.

Sinful Spirit

When the Bishop of Derry declared that the making, drinking or selling of poitín was a 'reserved sin', not all the Sperrin people were aware of the theological implications of 'reserved'. It was generally accepted that if you made, sold or drank poitín, you would have a confrontation with the Bishop in his mansion in Derry. Your alternative was eternity in a place even worse than the Sperrins.
Brendan O was a decent hardworking labourer, married to a zealous, devout, scrupulously Catholic lady, who discovered that Brendan, in a weak moment, had shared a drink of poitín with a neighbour.

She consulted the parish priest, who had no love for Brendan, and who told her unequivocally that Brendan was staring perdition in the face if he did not get absolution from his lordship. So Brendan disconsolate, guilty, regretful and reluctant, set off for Derry. 'He's away to Derry', the community learned, with that special delight which is reserved for mortification of neighbours.

Poteen Drinkers painting by Brian Whelan

When Brendan arrived after his first train journey, and with the help of many, many Derry citizens, who helped direct the helpless penitent to the Bishop's residence, he knocked on the door and was greeted by a familiar looking face, and an unexpected welcome. "Brendan, what are you doing here?" she was a neighbour's daughter working as a servant girl in the Bishop's palace. When he explained his mission, she told him, "The poor man is driven astray in the head with people like you. He can't sleep, his nerves are shot. I'm not going to let you near him." "What will I do?" said Brendan. "Go home," she answered. "But first, have you had anything to eat?" He admitted he was too nervous to eat before leaving home, and six hours later, had not broken fast. "Come into the kitchen and I'll make you a meal." she said.

When Brendan had finished his meal, he asked her, "What will I do?" "I'll tell the Bishop you were here," she said, "and that's all you need to do."

When he arrived back home, his wife asked him, "Did you see the Bishop?" and he replied "I didn't see the Bishop, but I saw the girl." In some townlands, "I saw the girl" soon became a euphemism for indicating avoidance of responsibility.

Holy Spirit

Glass was scarce after the First World War, and bottles were rare in the Sperrin mountains. A poitín maker called Taidg needed a glass bottle to fill an order. Unfortunately, he was unable to find a spare bottle anywhere in his townland and was forced to go to a very religious neighbour, who frowned on the production or consumption of poitín. When he asked her for a bottle, she replied she had only one bottle in the house, and that's where she kept her holy water. "And you're not getting that," she said.

Taidg, with a doleful expression, replied, "That's a pity. You see, the poitín is for the priest." The lady immediately responded, "In that case, I'll put the holy water in a bowl and you can have the bottle." The priest, of course, never saw the poitín or the bottle.

Weak Spirit

Johnny H, a small farmer from the Sperrins, was noted for a caustic wit. On one occasion, on a fair day, he and some friends went for a drink in a village pub. The owner of the pub was known to dilute some of his products. Hovering over his customers, he inquired, "Mr. H, would you like a little water in your whisky?" "No," said Johnny, "but could you take some of the water out of it?"

Funeral Spirit

Between the valleys of the Owenkillew and the Owenreagh rises the Sperrin mountain called Crocknamohill. One explanation for the name is as follows.

When funerals were held, it was common to carry the corpse over the mountain to the church at Badoney. On one occasion, a group escorting a coffin containing the body of a young boy over the mountain met another group returning from an internment earlier in the day. Both groups had consumed a lot of poitín and were noisy, belligerent and violent. A confrontation ensued and the fight lasted well into the evening. When it was over, it was decided that they would bury the coffin of the young boy right there on the mountain. Since that time, the mountain has been called Crocknamohill, the hill of the boy.

Secret Spirit

It was hard for publicans to sell poitín so they had to disguise it. One way was to mix the poitín with red wine and sell it as rum.

The smoke from turf fires in hidden glens where poitín was produced was a dangerous tell-tale sign that illicit distilling was in progress. The primus stove was a useful invention for the poitín maker, as the poitín could be produced with greater secrecy.

These two stories were related by another "Son of the Sperrins" but this time from Ballinascreen where "Mickey" was his fairly close neighbour.

Syruptitious Spirit

The use of the primus stove by Taidg of Tyrone leads us back to Ballinascreen where "Mickey", an innovative master of poitín-making, plied his trade close to the county march, during and after World War II. Mickey must have done some business with American soldiers stationed near Ballinascreen because he became the owner of an old 3-ring gas cooker courtesy of "the Yankees". This gave Mickey the decided advantage of abundant, reliable heat for his still with no tell-tale smoke. Another Mickey innovation was syrup instead of sugar in his process.

During one raid on Mickey's operation, as he watched them from his hiding place "up in the whuns", the police found empty Tate and Lyle tins and nothing else. The police, unable to pin him for poitín, charged him with poochin (poaching) and jailed him for 3 months.

Explosive Spirit

Mickey said he would never do jail time again, that he would shoot dead the next man that tried to put him away. The gun with which he would do the deed was also thanks to "the Yanks" and it got him into a bit of a pickle. One day when turning a stubborn lock with his left hand while holding the revolver "at the ready" in his right hand, the gun "went aff" and sent the bullet down along the outside of his leg and through the sole of his 'wellie'. He got Dr. Frank to dress his grazed leg, telling him that it was a cigarette he had dropped down there. Dr. Frank's diagnosis? "It must have been going very fast."

Mickey once buried five gallon drums of the 'quare stuff' in the heather but "some eejit" set fire to the heather. He couldn't send for the fire brigade because of the possible explosion which did eventually happen.

It would seem that he travelled by river as well as by road, and would tell his clients where a bottle might be 'found', should that be in a hedge, the river, or in an open field or even in the local graveyard (behind the headstone of a client's ancestors?).

Nocturnal Spirit

The first time I ever heard of poitín was when my father who was a **"Builder and General Ironmonger"** in Straw, told me about one cold, wet, windy night back in the 1940s, when there was an urgent knocking at our door. When he opened it, there was a local poitín maker (probably "Mickey"), down from the mountain, drenched to the bone, looking for a part or parts for his ailing still. I don't recall whether my father said he was able or willing to help mend Mickey's kettle or his worm (he didn't drink) but the sense of the clandestine nature of "the craetur" was brought vividly home.

Sperrin Spirit

It could have been one of Mickey's bottles that a big RUC man discovered in the suitcase of an in-law of mine, "Charlie", during a security search at Nutt's Corner or Aldergrove airport, many years ago. When asked what was in the bottle, Charlie thought it best to come clean and admitted that it was poitín. "Where did you get it?" said the RUC man. "Up in the Sperrins." was Charlie's reply. "Lucky man!" said the constable and waved him through.

Poetic Spirit

Did she read about history; did she read about Greece,
When Jason went searching for the Golden Fleece;
He came round by Broughderg by the foot of the hill,
Where Mickey Pat Roddy was running a still

I am sure that the boys got the best of the pot,
And there they sat down and they drank the whole lot;
They lit up their dudeens and talked about Greece,
And went off to Broughderg in search of the fleece.

Those lines from "The Wee Derry Pipe" (1982 version) by James O'Kane from Carntogher (in Swatragh) are the only *verses* we can find so far about poitín-*making* anywhere near the Ballinascreen area. ("Mickey Pat Roddy" is not the same "Mickey" as the one in the yarns mentioned above). In an earlier (1938) version of the same poem, Jason doesn't search in Broughderg but ...
He stopped at Slieve Gallon and under the hill
Discovered Pat Flannagan runnin' a still

Anonymous Spirit

Did "Miller Kane" get himself in trouble by naming "Mickey Pat Roddy"? A real person? "Pat Flanagan" fictional? There is 'still' a poitín-maker in Ballinascreen today whose fine mountain dew this editor has enjoyed, for scientific research purposes, don't ye know, but he/she shall remain nameless.

Non-Sectarian Spirit

There may not be many poems about poitín-*making*, in Ballinascreen. Neither of the local bards, Geordie Barnet or "Johnny Paul" Kelly drank, so they were not too interested in verse about illicit booze but one local-born bard who had emigrated, mentioned *potheen* and the "*ayther"* quite a few times in his verse. David Hepburn (born 1857 in Drumard) in his collection of poems which are pieced together as a long narrative called *The Kaylie*, used poitín, whiskey and "ayther" to fuel the wake-keening and crack-kaylie-ing that romps along in various metres with characters from different townlands coming together, both Protestant and Catholic, spouting verse in strong local Ballinascreen dialect, in "Tatty's" house in Drumard sometime during the 19th century. Tatty's house is reminiscent of "Joe Ned" Bradley's house in Ballybriest (in Lissan but closely tied to Ballinascreen) where it was, at a time in 1950s to the 1970s, a place for people who "dug with different feet" to enjoy some drink, crack and music.

Hepburn's *Kaylie* characters, Corick Sal, Denny Slow and Harry Gawt tell of prolonged, spirit-inspired, **pre**-wake "celebrations", parties and meetin's ...

> *Himself wis the boy that partuck of the joy-*
> *A house full av laughin' an'* **Ayther** *galore-*
> *Whin frens an' whin neighbours (an' shtrangers be jabers!)*
> *Drapp'd in till see Jacky M'Quade av Cahore.*
>   ...
> *So biddin' somebody fetch forrit the* **toddy**
> *An' missure it out with a noggin or bowl*
> *He toul' us till drink it, nor wan of us shrink it,*
> *By way av partin' shalute till his sowl.*

In "The Keenier's Lament for Jacky" ...

> *An' a score av the strongest, the stoutest, an' longest,*
> *Wir sint to the Cross for the* **whisky** *an' loaves.*
>   ...
> *'Twis thin whin their hearts all wir full, an' the quarts all*
> *Av* **potheen** *wir drunk, that the sintimint ran;*
>   ...
> *An' the divil another / Man chile or his mother*
> *Cud' av' hid more* **potheen** *from the light of the day.*

Even the priest arrived with all his liturgical gear ...

> *... An' a pint of the* ***"Best"*** *till put under his vest*
> *That he purchased that mornin' from Paddy McShane.*

Later in "Bracca" ...

> *The* **potheen** *in kegs wis rowl'd forrit, an' farls*

Tatty's house in Drumard.

School Spirit
Pedagogues and Poitín

Right there, wedged in between humdrum entries about teachers beginning their duties or retiring, in "The Schools of Ballinascreen (1823-1990)", a history of parish education by the late Fr Leo Deery P.P., is this seemingly incongruous entry from a newspaper article dated 16th of April 1897 ...

STILL HUNTING IN SPERRIN MOUNTAINS - ANOTHER SEIZURE OF POTEEN

> The poteen making fraternity, whose habitat is on the Sperrin Mountains near Draperstown, have fallen on evil days, and are gradually realizing the way of the transgressor is hard. Another revenue seizure has been made the other night, the seizing party upon this occasion being Seargent Stokes and Constable Cummins, Brown and McLein. The party arrived at the house of a man named Joseph McBride in the townland of Tullybrick, where a number of genial souls appeared to be making merry. Someone shouted, "There's the police!" but the warning came too late to secure the safety of the necessary tipple as there were the police with a vengeance, who at once seized upon 7 large bottles, each of which contained more or less poteen. This is the fourth seizure in the district within a short period of time.

What in God's name, has this to do with education, Father Deery? On further rummaging through your entries a few pages earlier, the mystery may be solved under "Bancran 1892"; " To help her numbers the Principal of the Girls' school, Mary Duffy, had been taking in boys to her infant girls' school. This annoyed the Principal of the Boys' school, *Joe McBride* ..." Surely you weren't suggesting in the juxtaposition of these notes that the principal of Bancran Boys' school was one of the merry, genial souls caught tippling poteen in Tullybrick not far from Bancran? You weren't, by any chance, piling it on when you also quoted this School Inspector in October 1894

> Have the teachers of the parish nothing better to do but sell bicycles, lamp oil, wire, be insurance agents, solicitors' clerks, agents for wool etc.? Conway of Draperstown school and McBride of Bancran school are in cahoots in most of these things ... The day you called at Bancran school, McBride was at a bicycle race in Belfast and left the school in charge of a monitor who is his own nephew. ... **They can make their own whiskey too** - they will soon start pawn shops ...

This Master McBride must have been the same one who in the early days of the 20th century would have visited McAllister's (then, O'Neill's, or earlier, McKeown's) spirit grocery in Straw to partake (legally) and take part in card games.

Still 'n All

Poteen
by Michael Longley

Enough running water
To cool the copper worm,
The veins at the wrist,
Vitriol to scorch the throat -

And the brimming hogshead,
Reduced by one noggin-full
Sprinkled on the ground,
Becomes an affair of

Remembered souterrains,
Sunk workshops, out-backs,
The back of the mind -
The whole bog an outhouse

Where, alongside cudgels,
Guns, the informer's ear
We have buried it -
Blood-money, treasure trove.

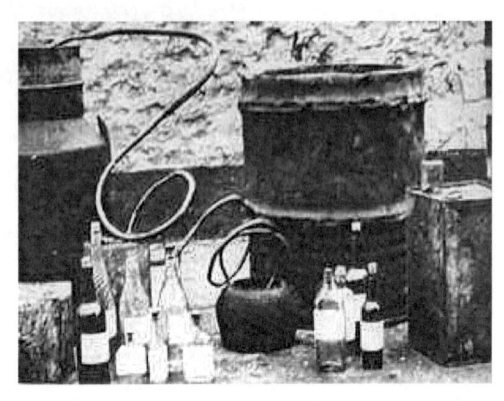

A fairly negative view of poteen-making from Belfastman, Michael Longley, but he touches on something that is often mentioned in the lore ...

The ***libation,*** *... one noggin-full/Sprinkled on the ground*, is as old as recorded history and it serves to reinforce the idea that spirits and religious ritual are inseparable.

What did a shebeen in the 'Screen look like? Erskine Nicol a Scottish painter who loved Ireland painted A Shebeen at Donnybrook in 1851. The fairs in the 'Screen may not have been as big as those around Dublin but no doubt its shebeens were just as lively as this.

The Doctor, the Priest and the Excise Man
The War on Drink

from The Irish Times Nov. 16, 2007

"The benefits of poteen and its history formed part of an engaging lecture last night at NUI Maynooth in a Science Week Ireland event. Poteen, Potions and Poisons was presented by senior lecturer in inorganic chemistry at the university, Dr Malachy McCann. His talk ranged from how spirit distillation came to Ireland, through the unexpected benefits of seriously toxic substances such as arsenic and cyanide. Poteen in chemical terms is little different to whiskey, vodka and other spirits produced through distillation. The resultant liquid has about 5 per cent alcohol and this is then repeatedly distilled to raise the percentage of alcohol. It is a brilliant antiseptic, excellent as a solvent to extract useful medicinal substances from plants, such as echinaecia, arsenic and cyanide in poultices and in certain anti-cancer treatments. Poteen can be made from a number of sources, including barley, potatoes and molasses."

Run like the divil from the excise man ...

Through the 1800s both state and church waged war on "the drink" in Ireland. Most of the medical profession would have long pointed out the obvious ill-effects of too much tippling but now the Church too turned its considerable power to the task of condemning all forms of imbibing whether legal or not and, as government became more entrenched, the reach of the excise man (right) extended deeper into the hills around Ballinascreen closing down stills and shebeens.

... and the priest

Father Theobald Matthew's crusade through the middle of the century had an especially great impact on the drinking habits of Ireland but not much is known about the number of teetotallers his work won over around Ballinascreen at that time. In the history of Ballinascreen parish by Rev. Coulter, he points out;

"Writers who describe Ballinascreen at the time [in first half of 1800's] are at one in paying tribute to the sobriety, hard work, and the kindliness of the parishoners"

Some ingenuity was exercised by the hard core drinking fraternity to get around tighter government restrictions, higher prices and church crusades on their favourite pastime. It may have begun with the dreaded "meths". Methyl alcohol, wood alcohol, methylated spirits, methanol. Cheap but deadly stuff by all accounts.

And then there was "the aethur" ...

Fear and Loathing in The Screen
... but we didn't inhale

Even though Draperstown was considered by many, including Ernest Hart, to be the *fons et origo mali* (the very source and origin of evil!) of ether drinking in the 19th century, there is no mention of inhaling it. It always seemed to have been drunk. Were the experiences of ether inhalation considered too extreme for the average south Derry tippler? Here is an account of the ether-inhaler experience from 1870's America.

> "*I once inhaled a pretty full dose of ether, with the determination to put on record, at the earliest moment of regaining consciousness, the thought I should find uppermost in my mind. The mighty music of the triumphal march into nothingness reverberated through my brain, and filled me with a sense of infinite possibilities, which made me an archangel for a moment. The veil of eternity was lifted. The one great truth which underlies all human experience and is the key to all the mysteries that philosophy has sought in vain to solve, flashed upon me in a sudden revelation. Henceforth all was clear: a few words had lifted my intelligence to the level of the knowledge of a cherubim. As my natural condition returned, I remembered my resolution; and, staggering to my desk, I wrote, in ill-shaped, straggling characters, the all-embracing truth still glimmering in my consciousness. The words were these (children may smile; the wise ponder): 'A strong smell of turpentine prevails throughout'*
> Oliver Wendell Holmes, Mechanism in Thought and Morals, Phi Beta Kappa address, Harvard Univeristy, June 29, 1870 (Boston: J.R. Osgood and Company, 1871).

Sounds suspiciously like the potion used to revive Finn McCumhaill. Or maybe its effects come close to what druids actually believed in. Dr. H Wadell refers to Ossian (a son of Fionn McCumhaill) and his beliefs, as found in his poetry, in a single deity which was how pure druidism saw the ultimate spirit ...

> "*All local gods to him were objects of ridicule. He recognized the Deity, if he could be said to recognize him at all, as an omnipresent vital essence, everywhere diffused in the world, centred for a lifetime in heroes. He himself, his kindred, his forefathers and the human race at large, were dependent solely on atmosphere; their souls were identified with the air, heaven was their natural home, earth their temporary residence and fire the element of purification, or the bright path to immortality for them when the hour of dissolution came. - The incremation of Malvina's remains, on the principle of transmutation and escape from the dark, perishable clay to luminous and immortal* **ether**, *is a beautiful illustration of this.*"

Incidentally of all the dangers associated with ether drinking, many of them exaggerated (it was actually less harmful to the metabolism than alcohol), the most dangerous was fire ..."*the principle of transmutation and escape from the dark"*. An ether induced explosive eructation near the hearth was a risky business; "it wouldn't do to rift into fire ... or the flames would travel down your throat", as one ether drinker put it. Another said that the drinker must mingle with care the pleasures of ether and tobacco, *"I knew a man that was always dhrinkin' it, and won day after a dose uv it, he wint to light his pipe and the fire cot his breath and tuk fire inside, and only for a man that was carryin' a jug of wather wud some whiskey to the kitchen, he'd a lost his life. He just held him down at wanst, as quick as he could, and poured down the wather down his throat."*

Most accounts of ether "huffing" (inhalation) by today's users point to it being as powerful as any drug-taking out there. In the Hunter S. Thompson novel *Fear and Loathing in Las Vegas* the character Raoul Duke (played in the film version by Johnny Depp) says,

"We had two bags of grass, seventy-five pellets of mescaline, five sheets of high-powered blotter acid, a saltshaker half-full of cocaine, and a whole galaxy of multi-colored uppers, downers, screamers, laughers... Also, a quart of tequila, a quart of rum, a case of beer, *a pint of raw ether*, and two dozen amyls. Not that we needed all that for the trip, but once you get into locked a serious drug collection, the tendency is to push it as far as you can. *The only thing that really worried me was the ether.* **There is nothing in the world more helpless and irresponsible and depraved than a man in the depths of an ether binge, and I knew we'd get into that rotten stuff pretty soon.**"

The sacred and the profane. The religious and the rotten. Why did this divinely depraved drug become so strongly associated with Draperstown to the point where it became known as the *fons et origo mali* of ether drinking, introduced to the town in 1846 or 1847 and for 13 years sold freely ... during the famine years? Why?

1. It was cheap ... at one sixth of the cost of whiskey.
2. For a time it was more readily available than alcohol ... and legal.
3. Illicit distillation of poitín was being stamped out.
4. It was believed to be good for various ailments.
5. One drink of it in the morning led to repeated intoxications through the day.
6. Intoxication was described as follows; *'In a few minutes, given an appropriate dose, the drinker's pulse quickened, his face flushed, a wave of perhaps hysterical excitement yielded to a calmer mood and "he dreamed himself into his personal paradise". He was in fairyland. Cares vanished in "blithesome gladness"; his pulse beat with joy, his eye glistened with love. You always heard music and you'd be cockin your ears at it ... you would see men climbing up the walls and going through the roof and down the walls nice and easy ..."*

Dr. Kelly's Remedy

A few years prior to the above date [1853] an unqualified medical man named Kelly practised at Draperstown and kept a drug store. He drank more whisky than was good for him; he was prevailed on to give up the whisky and then used ether and taught the people to use it also.

Dr. F. Auterson
quoted in
"EtherDrinking"
by Ernest Hart

For generations the Kellys of Ballinascreen have been known for their unqualified success in the fields of medicine, education and intoxication and here we have a Doctor Kelly in the 19th century, who may have been an ancestor of the author of this learned book, (as unqualified as his proud descendant in all of those arts) unselfishly aiding the good people of Draperstown in their quest for not just a better, healthier life, free from hangovers, liver complaints and bad consciences, but for the ultimate mystical union with the universe, its dark energy and dark matter, its great black, empty nothing that's really something, by instructing them in the fine art of partaking of "the ether". All the sources point to this excellent gentleman as the discoverer of the unqualified benefits of ingesting ether and to Draperstown as the very centre of its useage. Around 1850, at the height of Father Matthew's campaign to eradicate the scourge of drink, this other pioneer, at great risk to himself, achieved an unqualified breakthrough in his experiments with a volatile but guilt-free alternative to the evil whisky. Who knows how many days and weeks of whisky withdrawal symptoms he had to endure, how many intestinal eructations he had to withstand, how many hitherto uncharted fields of consciouness he traversed, how many near-death experiences from self-immolation he survived, how many scoffing insults he absorbed from the qualified who feared, with all their qualifications, to tread where he so bravely set foot? His unqualified devotion to the betterment of the bodies and souls of his fellowmen and women (and children) is an example to all of us who may be similarly unqualified.

"Adverse effects of ether drinking included profuse salivation, epigastric burning, and "rather violent eructations." In addition, several injuries and deaths were reported when ether drinkers were set on fire after being too close to open flames or when lighting a pipe. Early during the history of ether, the route of elimination was thought to be the lungs because the absence of an ether odor in urine made the kidneys an unlikely route for elimination." (from *Ether Drinking* by Ernest Hart)

Now we move on to another Kelly of a later generation, a poet of the pubs of Screen ...

"Paul Johnnie"
by Johnny Paul Kelly

There's a gentleman lives in this place,
We know him very well,
Paul Johnnie is this hero's name
We are not ashamed to tell.

He quarrelled with his people,
O'er the fortunes of a will,
And he went to live with decent folk,
Beside the Sixtowns mill.

For five long years of honest toil,
He served this gentleman,
Who gave him house and keeping,
Of the best in any land.

One lovely harvest evening,
Just as the sun went down,
He heard his master had been killed,
In a field beyond the town.

He washed his face and combed his hair,
And trimmed his shoe and sock,
And on starting for the village,
Took his wee alarm clock.

To get her put in order,
Just to know the time of night,
For he knew a handy fellow there,
Could easy put her right.

Vexation came upon him as,
He plodded o'er the stiles'
And to help a man in trouble,
He went in a while to **Myles.**

Says Myles, "This is a fearful case"
Says Paul, "I do agree,
And I hope he is shining happy,
He was always good to me.

"I brought my little timepiece,
I can hold her by my side,
If I get the length of Draperstown,
I will leave her with **McBride.**

Two days and nights to heavy grief,
He mourned him up and down,
He drunk a share and spent a share,
And toured around the town.

Until at length unhappy,
He resolved to turn home,
And see the little cabin,
And the cat he left at home.

And to bring his little timepiece,
He being in a sour frame,
He found that she was scuttled,
Where no one could name her name.

To search the public houses,
Of the village one and all,
He started down at **Thomas Quinn's,**
To give him the first call.

"Did you see my little ticker?"
"Well I will look and grope,
But you would not know between her,
And a pound of Hudson's soap."

He came back to **Mickey Kelly's,**
And says they, "Get out of here,
If you rise a row among us,
You will get one solid year."

Patrick Rodgers had his eye out,
And he knew his step was long,
"Yes," said he, "I see him coming,
There is something terror wrong."

"Did you see my little timepiece?"
"Well," said he, "she is not here."
But he spoke him very kindly,
"Give a call at **McAleers'**."

He was standing in the doorway,
With his face a little thin,
There was flour on his waistcoat,
And gravy on his chin.

"Did you see my little timepiece?"
"You have better take a walk,
Or I'll leave where they toe mark,
Around the ring of chalk."

He came back to **Charlie Harry's,**
And his gait was rather curt,
Said he, "I'm not so badly'
When they didn't take my shirt."

"Go round to **Paddy Hegarty,**
He is honest, he is good,
He will tell you all about it,
If you get him in that mood."

He went up to **Mark McKenna's**
And he told his story there,
Said he, "You need a woman, Paul,
To keep you in repair.

He went out upon the High Street,
And he cursed the village well,
He prayed it might be keeping time,
For someone down in hell.

This is but one adventure,
Of the many changing ways,
Through a happy roving lifetime,
That he spent for all his days.

If his history all was written,
As it properly should be,
It might lie beside O'Connell's
In the National Libaree.

Paul Johnnie's Crawl

(Photograph of street with labels: McAleer's, Thomas Quinn's, Patrick Rogers, Mickey Kelly's, Paul Johnnie himself?, Miles's)

Thirties Time Traveller

That mysterious poem by Johnny Paul Kelly is the only verse, until now, that we know of that name drops many of the pubs in the Draperstown of his day, in the 1920's or 30's when Kelly was in his poetic prime. The hero/narrator, in mourning over his dead master, had presumably been 'waking' and drowning his sorrows in the town over two days and nights and lost his wee, broken alarm clock in the process so he had to revisit all the pubs that he might have been in to try and find it. Was Paul in an intoxicated timewarp like Cú Chulainn on his crawl through The Screen. Had time stopped? Why were some of the publicans so unhelpful and even rough on him? What shenanigans had he been up to? Why did McKenna say he needed a woman to keep him "in repair"? Is this a below-the-belt *double entendre* crack about his "little timepiece" being in need of repair?

Quinn's, Mickey Kelly's, Patrick Rogers, McAleers', Charlie Harry's, Paddy Hegarty, Mark McKenna's and Miles's are all mentioned. *McBride* did not refer to a pub but to a handy man with clocks. By the way, Johnny Paul Kelly, the poet, was not a drinker and did not frequent pubs. Maybe Paul Johnnie is his bibulous alter ego.

Only one of these publicans' names survives in the pub-owning fraternity of today; *McKenna* of the Railway Bar and that is at the moment closed, so in the 70 - 80 years since it was written, all but one have changed families and shape-shifted or are no longer pubs. *Thomas Quinn's* became The Burnside Bar (Fullen's), *Mickey Kelly's* - now the Bank of Ireland, *Patrick Rogers* - owned a pub in the building which is now David O'Kane's newsagent's shop. *McAleers'* - now the Apparo Restaurant (still licensed), *Charlie Harry's* - ?, *Paddy Hegarty* ? *Miles's* was demolished in the late 1950's and the site redeveloped a number of times by the Burns family.

Closing Time

*Yeah, we're drinking and we're dancing
but there's nothing really happening
The place is dead as Heaven on a Saturday night ...*
from *Closing Time*
by Leonard Cohen

7 of the 8 pubs mentioned in the poem by Johnny Paul Kelly are no longer in operation and a further 4, not mentioned, are also extinct; Brown's, Hudie's (McCullagh's), Molly Murray's and Toner's. A grand total, a nice round figure, of 2 dozen known pubs existed in the parish at one time or another over the last 100 years or so.
According to this Daily Mirror letter exchange back in the 1980's, the parish had 15 pubs in operation at that time.

J.T Stephenson Boxtree Rd, Harrow Weald, Middlesex asks:
Q. *Biggleswade, Beds., was reckoned 50 years ago to have more pubs per head of the population than anywhere else. Is this still a fact?*
A. *No. Biggleswade now has 12 pubs for 12,100 people but Draperstown, Co Londonderry, Northern Ireland, used to boast 15 pubs for 500. Canterbury, Kent has one for every 293 people.*

In the South Derry and District 1902 almanac 12 publicans are listed for Draperstown; Patrick Bradley, P. Connor, Francis Convery, Robert Ferguson, Michael Kelly, Patrick Morris, Michael McAleer, J. McNamee, Patrick O'Kane, T. Quin, B. Rodgers and Michael Toner. In the 1909 almanac P. Bradley, Connor, Morris and J. McNamee are gone but M. Bradley, Mark McKenna, Miles McNamee, S. O'Kane, Jahmes O'Neill, James Sweney and M. Wilson are added for a total of 15 publicans serving a population of 487 (1901 census).

At the time of a trial printing of this book in 2008, 15 pubs were still alive (though some were dozin') and nearly a dozen were done for, dead. 3 of the 15 licences were for new establishments which are not strictly "pubs". Since then at least 5 have closed permanently or temporarily. 15 may have been the largest number going at any one time although it is possible that anywhere up to 24 could have been operating simultaenously *in "Greater" Ballinascreen* in the late 1800s perhaps. Whatever the statistics, even the fairly certain 15 is a formidable number of drinking establishments for any town of 500 people, anywhere in the world. Surely Draperstown holds or held the record. Oddly enough The Guinness Book of World Records does not seem to have this category.

Let us go back and look at the half-forgotten pubs beginning with those still standing. Throughout these 'histories' you will notice family names appearing and reappearing. Different pubs were owned or run by related families. To this day there are family connections between these old pubs and today's bars.

1. Brown's

You can still see the name fairly clearly above the door of this lonely bar at the corner of Bancran Road and the road to Cranagh and Plumbridge. It closed sometime in the 1960's as many small outlying pubs did, a time when getting to the pub no longer was by shank's mare but by car, an unfortunate change in drinking habits which probably led to many accidents and brought about the demise of these small local bars. Below - Brown's bar today, the sorry end of some of these old pubs.

2. Hudie's (McCullagh's)

Another 'outlier' pub, like Brown's, this one on the Doon Road, sometimes known as McCullagh's. This was a very lively place back in the 1960's with plenty of young people and singing galore. It was far enough away from the most frequented pubs to be a haven for the more discerning drinkers who did not find the growing "lounge culture" to their taste.

3. Mickey Paul's (Kelly's)

Yet another outlying townland pub. Nothing left of the old place except this view of the rolling hills of Ballinascreen that the drinker of old might have seen, if fit to see, as he or she came out the front door of Mickey Paul Kelly's Doon pub which has the distinction of being the only Ballinascreen pub to get blown up during the "troubles". Mickey's descendants now live in a fine new bungalow on the actual site. It was the favourite pub of the young ones of the 1950's and 60's when Joe McAllister remembered some fine nights there with John Leyden and Joe Convery singing "oul songs". "Mickey Paul" was no relation of the poet "Johnny Paul" Kelly whose poem sparked all this.

4. Miles's (1)

The only photo we have of Pat Miles's pub is this one above, a still taken from Fr Mick Kelly's film of a Straw church visit by the bishop of Derry, in the late 1940s. Note the bunting for 'Wee Buns'. Pat lived in the two storey house on the right and the pub and shop (spirit grocery) would have been in the lower (one storey?) section partly hidden to its left. This is what it looked like when old Pat "Miles" McNamee was still living there or, later, when McAllisters used it as a shed and a place to bottle Guinness. It is now gone of course, flattened in the late fifties to make a parishoner parking lot on the opposite side of the road from Straw chapel gates.

The premises changed hands a number of times. From 1890 to 1910 Jim Kelly, a descendant of the Mickey Eoghain Kellys, many of whom still live around Ballinascreen, rented the premises from the then owner Hughie Bradley and ran a 'spirit grocers' here ... the same Bradleys who owned the Shepherds Rest before the Doyles. Hughie was a grand uncle of Kevin Kelly who still lives in Straw and who was able to tell us that Hughie had bought it from the O'Hagans who had lived there for generations.

It was a thriving, go-ahead kind of business at one time, a builder's yard in the back with timber and steel for sale and rented out to various enterprises: e.g. Willie Smith had a carpenter's shop and made wheels for carts and traps. There may even have been a cobbler's shop. Jim was a good business man, making it the main business in Straw. He later built his own shop and house where his grandson, Seamus still lives, opposite the end of Shanmullagh lane. In its final days during Pat Miles's time it would be open for only a day in the year just to keep the licence active.

Around 1930 Miles McNamee, bought it from Bradley after he had sold up in Draperstown (see Conville's) and lived here as well as operating the spirit grocer's. Joseph McAllister said that when Miles ran the the bar it was a "very warm" pub, no draughts, a good potbellied stove for heating, much more comfortable than McAllister's own bar at that time. When Miles died, his brother Pat left the homeplace in Glengamna to take it over, living there with his two sisters. This was where he, too, died.

I can remember visiting Pat in the company of my father some time in the early 1950s. Pat was bedridden by then, in a small, sunlit back bedroom. There seemed to be plenty of dogs and cats to keep him company. Off to the right of the building was a fairly high wall and behind it an orchard where we, as kids will, helped ourselves to plums while keeping a wary eye out for old Pat who could still manage to rouse himself and come out to chase us away in his longjohns and to fire a warning shot above the trees with his double barrelled shotgun. Pat's dogs seemed to spend most of their time sitting out in front of the building and howling at the Angelus bell. When Pat died they didn't need the bells. They howled for days, in mourning.

I can also remember playing around the building later in the 1950s, finding a set of weigh-scales and old receipts for groceries still in the drawers behind the counter of the spirit grocer end of the building; bread for 1d ... one penny. Mickey Kelly and I helped Peter McAllister bottle, label and cap Guinness there at the end of the era when local bars were permitted to do bottling and have their own names on the label. Memory may be playing tricks here but this is what the label may have looked like. The McAllister name did appear on a number of beverages but it may have been "McAllisters, Ballymena" a firm (not related to the Straw family) that delivered minerals, beers and spirits all over mid-Ulster.

As the building deteriorated the rats took over. I will always associate the huge rats I saw there, through a hole in a wall at the back, with the old yarn about Matha Kielt saying he had seen "rats with wrists as thick as my tail". And since the rats might have had access to some spilled extra stout, there was also the association to the wish of the porter-drinking man that he would like to have been a rat in Guinness's brewery where it was said that many a rat was drowned in a vat.

This from one ex-Straw correspondent who went to the school opposite it, in the sixties,*"I remember it as a decrepit building when I was at primary school - and I also remember that Peter McAllister briefly opened it and called it the 'You Drop Inn' or maybe the 'U Drop Inn' - and even put that sign on it, but I don't think this was a serious commercial venture on his part - more a tongue in cheek in-joke for the McAllister regulars. I think maybe they even had some music there at weekends?"*

5. Miles II (later Conville's)

Bards and Barmen

Conville may have been the last family to run a licensed premises here, right at The Cross, probably the most strategically situated piece of real estate in the early days of Draperstown. Was this where Laughlin McNamee set up his headquarters? Was this the spot where a cattle dealer could take his glass in comfort? Evidence that this might be the real "spiritual" birthplace of Draperstown can be found in the postcard below, from the 1920s. The sign above the door of the building on the right reads, "Miles McNamee Wine and Spirit Merchant".

This Miles might be a descendant of Laughlin the real founder of An bothar buí, "the Yellow Road" that would later become Draperstown. Could the founding father have had any better vantage point to watch over the Fair Day and over the growing town "around his door" while raking in some good money selling liquor to flush farmers every First Friday?

In John O'Donovan's letters written at the same time as his survey of 1836 another McNamee is mentioned, one who had helped him with stories about old Ballinascreen ...

"... Provost Lord John Eldon McNamee, *Inn-Keeper*, Draperstown-cross, the descendant of the bard ... to McLaughlin ..."

McLaughlin was one of the local chiefs who fought the chief O'Neill and lost not only the battle but also the Bard McNamee who then became The O'Neill's bard after stepping on the carcass of his previous employear. O'Neill was to pay for bardic services but McNamee never got a farthing. The bard provoked one bad tempered brother of The O'Neill with word play. "Are you punning me?" says this O'Neill, threatening to hang the bard for his disrespect but the wily McNamee managed to fool his victim into hanging not him but The O'Neill's own son. After writing this tale O'Donovan rails at this kind of savagery of the native Irish and at the "sacred Bard, a low, mean, and unprincipled renegade".

So here we have a bardic family becoming, in later generations, inkeepers. From poets to publicans! It wouldn't be a surprise to find that the McNamees had in an even earlier age been druids.

The "Provost Lord" must have been an earlier (than Miles) descendant of Laughlin whose name might suggest the earlier McLaughlin loyalty. These McNamees seem to be a different family from the one that ran the nearby "hotel" mentioned in the later "**the shamrock**" section. Miles McNamee sold up sometime in the late 1920's to the Convilles and started the spirit-grocer business in Straw covered in the earlier "Miles's (I)" page.

6. Molly Murray's

My own brother Brendan's favourite bar back in the 1940s. He and his friends frequented Molly's when it was in its heyday. I wish I'd recorded some of his stories about the place. At one time Molly plied her trade out of what was McKenna's Railway Bar (probably where she was in my brother's day) until she moved her business to where you could still see (in 2009) the old window with her name on it near the Meeting House. Molly's bar, wherever she served, always had a warm atmosphere. The building was a private house for a few decades, then was vacant and almost derelict for some years but is now being renovated. Below; one of the late Paddy Heron's 1960s photos of the houses and shops across from the Diamond. Paddy would eventually set up shop himself beside Molly Murray's in the 'legal drugs' business.

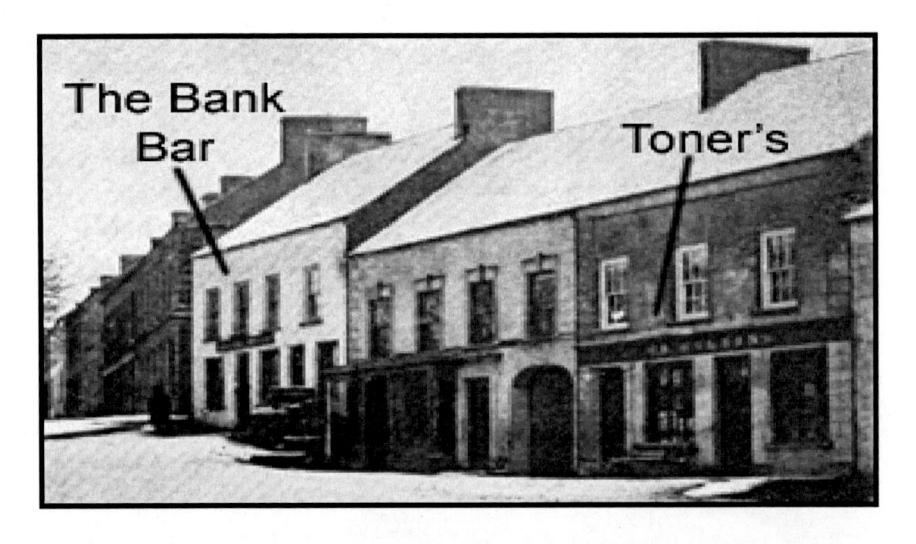

7. Toner's/Wilson's/Mullan's

The building is still there but is now Laurie O'Kane's chemist shop. In the old postcard (above) taken on a rare snowy day in Draperstown you can just make out the name "Wilson" on the shopfront on the extreme right. "M. Wilson" is listed as the publican in 1909 almanac but the formidable widow, Annie Wilson is in the 1901 census, presumably "M's" widow (from Tyrone) who spoke both Irish and English, a "farmer and spirit merchant" with 2 children. 10 years later she is recorded as being a "publican and grocer". This would have been Michael Toner's pub before and/or after the Wilson days. At one stage it was Patsy Mullan's pub. Now it is O'Kane's Chemist shop licensed to purvey drugs other than alcohol.

8. Mickey Barney's (Kelly's)

I remember, back in the 1950s, seeing "M. Kelly" (or M.B. Kelly?) on the sign where the "Bank of Ireland" is now, so at one time there were two pubs side-by-side here on St Patrick's Street, with Regan's Market Bar to the left of this. In the 1901 census there is a 56-year-old Michael Kelly "spirit merchant" at these premises. In 1911 he was listed as "publican and grocer". He and his wife Jane had 6 children but only 2 daughters survived to 1911.

9. McKenna's (Railway Tavern)
The First Station of The Cross

The most recent casualty of the change in drinking habits of many people in the area is The Railway Tavern. The bar itself is closed but the licence is still active in the form of the "off licence". Sadly, the "historic" sign has been removed. This was one of the most 'respected' bars in Draperstown and one with a long history. Being so close to the terminal of the now defunct rail link to Magherafelt and beyond, gave it some genuine prestige through its history. Since a 'tavern' was not just a drinking establishement but a place for travellers to rest and lodge, were there rooms to rent on the premises? When the rail link closed in 1950, The Tavern's glory days were probably over. The bus that replaced the train eventually had its terminal down at the Cross outside McNamee's pub, so up here on High Street was no longer the place for travellers to sup.

The local McKenna family name has long been associated with this and other drinking establishments in the area and beyond with a Henry McKenna emigrating to Kentucky in 1837 and eventually founding a distillery there which grew into a major business continued by his sons. The company was eventually bought by Seagrams but the Henry McKenna name lives on and bourbon of that name is still very much available in America. The whole story of the McKenna whiskey distilling empire can be found in Angela O'Keeney's *Looking Back on Ballinascreen.*

It may not be to everyone's liking that one of the most successful businessmen sons of Ballinascreen in the U.S.A. was a distiller of bourbon whiskey. (It turns out Henry was not of the same McKenna family that ran The Railway Tavern but from one that lived in the building that is now the Ulster Bank.)

In its final years The Tavern was the haunt of a few local business people and a place to bring visitors such as returning emigrants. Locals and visitors who would normally avoid local pubs because they had a regular clique clientele would make an exception for The Railway Tavern. It was a place of conversation, without music or the lounge atmosphere that became the norm in the 1970's and later. The late John Burns who was one of the most respected businessmen in the area through the last half of the 20th century, was a regular here. Maybe when he died, so did The Tavern.

The "old world dignity" of The Railway Tavern is evident in the photos here (courtesy of Shane Kelly). I can remember being in the snug on the left with "sport of kings" enthusiast, the late John Burns, sitting in one of those chairs, as we listened to his yarns about the horse races in various parts of Ireland.

10. The Rural College - The Mountview

One of the shortest-lived bars in Ballinascreen, the Mountview was part of The Derrynoid Centre or "Rural College", opened to great fanfare and with great expectations back in 1995, closing recently at the end of 2011. The grounds of the College had a much longer history as the site of the home of "The Big House" belonging to Judge Torrens who played a large part in the Planter settlement of Draperstown. So the Mountview Bar lasted some 16 years and for a time was a very busy "hotel bar" when the College was host to conventions with guests coming from all over Ireland and beyond.

11a. Moyola Bar (Cuskeran's)
Resurrected ~ see Apparo

It looked a downright derelict mess in 1969 (left) but the Moyola was well situated and a local Hegarty restaurateur brought the old place back from the brink.

132

Still Serving

The rest of this book looks at the 14 pubs of Ballinascreen that were still doing business as of late 2012. (2 of them are now in limbo)

11b. Moyola ... Apparo
No horses here now.

      This could be the last of 11 pubs in the "Closing Time" section but it is now transformed into Draperstown's only(?) Euro-chic restaurant and hotel with an international reputation, The Apparo (which means, in Greek, "no horse"; in Latin "prepare, make ready, furnish, provide"!), a far cry from the days in the mid 1960s when I served behind the bar of the Moyola (the most evocative name in Screen bars) during the summer months, a raw recruit of Mickey Cuskeran's and his brother Matt. At that time Frankie and Michael McAleer were still living in the quarters at the rear of the pub as this had previously been their family's ***"McAleer's"*** pub mentioned in Johnny Paul Kelly's poem "Paul Johnnie". In those days there were probably many horses tethered outside this well-situated establishment. In the 1960s it looked a bit like the photo opposite. When the bar was opened in the morning the smell of stale stout and smoke would have fairly knocked you down. On a busy Fair Day the punters often had to sit on stout cases since very few chairs or tables were provided in the area to the left of the door. The bar was behind the bigger window. It was a rough and ready establishment in those days where I got to meet a number of the well-known characters among the Ballinascreen serious drinking fraternity whose members would hardly be welcomed on the premises today. The Apparo, then, is our transitional watering hole between the "Closing Time" pubs and the "Still Serving"

Regan's in 2003. It has not changed much in the last 40 years. The "booky's" next door was the bettor's friend and/or enemy for over 60 years.

> "When money's tight and hard to get
> And your horse has also ran,
> When all you have is a heap of debt -
> A pint of plain is your only man."
>
> Flann O'Brien

On this day in 2006, it was not Leeds on the telly but Ireland under Mick McCarthy who got John Joe saluting. Neither Leeds nor Ireland have done much since but for John Joe it's a case of "Marching on together"

12. Regan's
United Forever

This pub is often referred to locally as "John Joe's" and there's no doubt about who runs the show here. A shrine to Leeds United is what greets the punter as he enters this hallowed hall. As far back as I can remember John Joe Bradley was a Leeds supporter even when we were both nippers running around Straw school in the mid-1950s when he and I were probably the only scholars there, interested in the English "Football Association" which would have been frowned upon in some quarters. His hero was, and still is, Welshman John Charles the "Gentle Giant", and John Joe has been to Elland Road often enough to be considered a true Leeds man. He has always bucked the GAA trend in Ballinascreen and bravely supported local soccer in Draperstown for a good part of his adult life. He managed a soccer team called Draperstown United in the mid-1960s and, later helped Draperstown Celtic which is still going today.

With the "SP" (Starting Price) "bookie's office" attached, you would have to consider this bar not just a soccer shrine but a horse-racing one too, the obvious, convenient place to go to celebrate a win on the horses or drown sorrows on a loss or watch the races on TV, although the racing connection has faded over the years. Before the legalization of off-track betting in the early 1960s there had been a bookie's in "The Shammels" but it was a clandestine affair. Michael Regan bought the pub here on the Derrynoid Road and started the first legal bookie shop in Draperstown in a lean-to, corrugated-roofed shed attached to the premises on the same spot it is today. You can see the smaller, earlier version in the 1969 photo (below). Martin O'Kane was the first bookie, a sharp man with the numbers. Mick Regan's son, Kevin, took over as the bookie in the late 60s but double tragedy overtook the Regan family within a few short months when, first, Mick died on Boxing Day 1968 and Kevin died in a car accident in February '69. Kevin's sister, the late Eithne Regan, came back from England and took over the position of bookie. She married John Joe some years later and he has run the pub since. Previous barmen included Hughie Traynor and Olly Crosset. In recent decades the bookie business lost much of its gritty personal touch with the installation of automated betting machines and as of 2013 the booky shop at this location was closed, having moved to a High Street location.

13. the shamrock

One of the oldest bars in Draperstown has changed hands (through leasing) many times over the years, so quickly lately, it's hard to keep up! It is now known as **the shamrock** (as of summer 2013) after having been **ned kelly's** for about a year. For a while, we thought "The Kelly Gang" was back in town during 2012. When Jim Kelly and Mickey "Barney" Kelly (back in the early 20th century) and then Denis Kelly and Mickey Paul Kelly in the 1970s all got out of the bar business, there was not a single "Kelly" pub left in a parish coming down with Kellys, for some 30 years. Sean Kelly of Straw, Paddy "Brian" Kelly's son was the proprietor of this storied old place, as close to "The Cross" of Laughlin McNamee's original premises as it is possible to get. **the shamrock** is run by John Mulligan of the same family as the Drumderg *Mulligan's Bar*. It has a patio and features music groups like *JD Country* and *Bleedin' Cowboys*.

Through the 1950s and 60s the bar was known simply as *"McNamee's"*. Michael and Denis McNamee would have been the publicans. In the 2000s era it was run by the Groogan family who had made it an intimate, comfortable sportsbar known as **Over the Bar** and before that the Donnelly family ran it for some years. In this heavily retouched, almost painted postcard (below) of a 1909 parade day in Draperstown you can just make out part of the words "McNamee Hotel" high on the gable of the white building to the right, the gable of today's "**the shamrock**" now abutted by *Johnny's Amusements*. There is still a strong McNamee connection in building-owner Jim Heron, married to Margaret McNamee, daughter of Johnny and a niece of Denis and Michael.

Right; "McNamee's" when it was run by the Donnelly family. 2003 photo, courtesy of Isabel Hegarty whose photos helped start this 'record' of the pubs of Ballinascreen.

Above; a Paddy Heron photo of the transportation hub of Draperstown around McNamee's in the 1950s, including Molly McGuigan's wee shop that served as the Number 112 bus station 'lounge' and snack bar! Below; Denis McNamee behind the bar back in the 1950s or 60s. Photo, courtesy of Michael McNamee, his nephew.

14. The Market Inn
The Nineteenth Hole

Perhaps the busiest bar in Draperstown with a wide range of clientele, farmers, teachers, businessmen, golfers, students, tourists, clerics ... you name it. It has a good restaurant and lively music scene. It has kept up with the times but also kept to its roots.

From the Market Inn's own website;

The Market Inn began its life as a farmers' pub back in the days of spirit grocers, but the present family, the Regans, have been keeping the fun going for more than half a century. Run by the present owner's father – Brendan Regan from 1947, his son Maurice Regan has been at the pumps since 1987.

In the past twenty years a number of refurbishments have taken place, with the latest re-fit completed in June 2007. Good news often travels by word-of-mouth and apparently the word about the Market Inn has travelled as far as Boston – two members of the Kennedy family are known to have had a drink or two at the bar.

The Market Inn has always been identified with the sporting life of the community, and there is a flourishing golf society based in the Market Inn. "Don't worry about being conscripted into any of these energetic activities if you call in for refreshments and directions. I never do" – says Owen Kelly (local journalist and broadcaster). "I just go for the craic. The Market Inn has an ordained role in the scheme of things as a forum for the discussion of the great questions of the day, such as the price of turkeys or where flies go in the wintertime."

Maurice Regan also says ... *"Mickey Barney's was another pub right beside me where the Bank Of Ireland now is and they also kept wool at the back. Regans has been owned by the family since 1947 and previously by a Joseph Toner (from Brackagh I think). The oldest date I have of his ownership was 1929 He died around 1945 and it was sold on in 1947.*

My father, Brendan Regan died July 31st 1971 and the bar was then run by Charlie Rodgers. Charlie had himself an untimely death in 1987. He was at the digging of his brothers grave when it subsided in Moneyneena and he fell in and was killed. (Charlie was a barman for 50 years between here and Belfast) I have been at the helm since 1987."

Inn Habit

During Brendan Regan's time, probably in the 60s, the Nazareth nuns used to leave collection boxes in the bar and came around once in a while to collect the proceeds. The nuns were about to go in when a 'kind' 'gentleman' (we're not sure if it was Jamie 'postman' Lagan or Martin O'Kane) approached and said, *"Sisters, there's a lot of farmers in there. As it's the fair day and the language wouldn't be great, if you go in through the main door and turn left into the snug, I'll get Mr Regan to attend to you."* The nuns duly obliged and the 'kind gentleman' went into the bar and told Brendan's nephew, Niall Regan, who would have done a few shifts in the bar in those days, *"There's two businessmen after going into the snug for a private chat and they want 'Two monks by the neck'"* and the story goes that Niall pulled two bottles of *Monk* beer, headed for the snug and the 'kind gentleman' made a hasty retreat before the fan took an unsavoury hit!

One of the other legends of this Regan's Bar was the late Emmet O'Kane who would break into poetry at the drop of a hat, or the drop of anything. He had a genius for ad lib rhyming in the very old Gaelic tradition of satirizing friends and foes alike.

Above; the big staff of the Market Inn needed on a busy night. Right; the late John Joseph O'Hagan behind what was not his typical tipple (a wee Bush).

Hot times (above) outside the Inn during a busking festival and inside it (left) for the annual Arthur's (Guinness) Day.
A number of events and music groups are shared by various pubs on Draperstown's main street, including Market Inn and Corner House.

15. The Corner House

The Corner House sponsors Cancer Care fund raisers, darts competition and much more. Below; JD Country and a group of Corner House folk.

15. The Corner House

Always known as **"Mary Pat's"** through the 1950's-70's, it would have been the "best-looking" bar in the town and it still is. All the makeovers that it has gone through have managed to preserve its fine exterior architectural flourishes. In the 1979 architectural heritage book *Moneymore and Draperstown* the above photo is the only one of any pub in the town. The caption by author James Stevens Curl reads, *"Sophisticated Italianate stucco-work at Draperstown, probably influenced by Booth or even John Allen"*

During the 1980's Francis Kelly owned it, turning it into a popular restaurant and club and calling it the **Corner House**. I don't know if Francis was into Italianate stucco-work but his earthy humour added its own fine flourishes!

In 1990 the McAlary family bought it from Francis and have owned it since though they leased it out at times over the years to Brian McGurk ('95-'97) and Vincent Hurl ('97-2006) when it was called **Talk of the Town**. When Walsh's hotel group leased it in 2008 they revived the **Corner House** name and tried to rebuild its club music atmosphere. It wasn't until the McAlary owners (Tracey and Hugh, her father) took the reins again that it got fully back on track. Tracey tells us that it has been renovated and expanded in the upper floors where a restaurant and function room can serve 50+ people, making it the busiest restaurant in the town. Weekends are lively with sponsored dart competitions, busking festivals, "Sunset Rallys" and "Truck Pulls" while pop and country music groups like *Ciaran and Debra, Shelbies, Bleedin' Cowboys, Tiny Lions, JD Country* and *Keep 'er Lit*, all keep the singing and dancing going. (photos p.141)

An old yarn going back to an earlier era had some tourist sophisticates finding their way into the **Corner House** for a meal. Before ordering dinner they asked the waitress for the wine list. The manager was called for and he told them, "I don't have a wine list but here's a bottle of 'Bó Jealous Pis'."

Various owners of the venerable **Corner House** *have redesigned the facade of what is perhaps the best-looking bar in Ballinascreen, maintaining its heritage character above in 2003 (Vincent Hurl ran it from 1997-2006) and below left in 2008. Photo below right shows Skibereen performing there as have many other folk and rock groups over the years.*

16

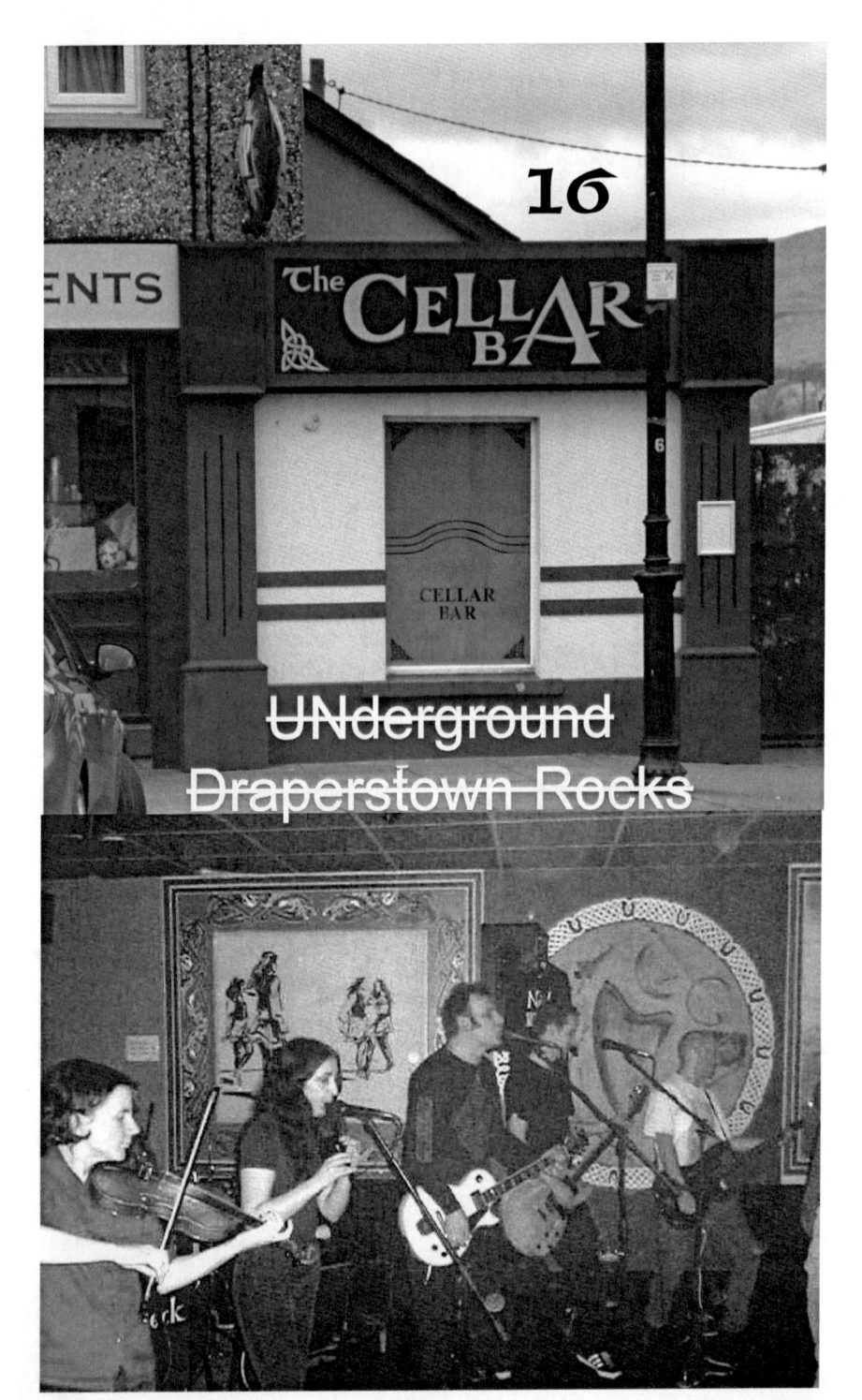

UNderground
Draperstown Rocks

The CELLAR BAR

ST. PATRICK'S STREET
DRAPERSTOWN

THE HEART OF LOCAL MUSIC

WWW.CELLARBAR.INFO
WWW.MYSPACE.COM/CELLAR_BAR
FOR FREE WEEKLY GIG UPDATES SIMPLY TXT 'CELLARBAR' TO 82055

Not exactly a stellar-looking bar on the outside but one with a stellar history in the field of music especially in recent years. It is well known around the world for its lineup of new rock, alternative music and traditional Irish. The Glasgowbury music festival held out in Moneyneena filters various groups down here to the Cellar Bar for groundbreaking performances ... the "G-sessions". It's a young, vibrant crowd most of the time and they pass on the word on My Space and Youtube putting The Cellar Bar and Draperstown on the map as the centre of cutting edge Ulster music.

The underground music scene of today's Cellar Bar or "Funker's Bunker" is a long way away from the days of Willie McShane (left and below left). There's something almost spiritual about this scene. The suited, teetotal Willie with his Pioneer pin, like a priest (druid?), gracefully, ritually pouring a bottle of stout, surrounded by the neat, serried ranks of spirits in their discreetly wrapped bottles. Prior to 1922 this bar was originally part of a spirit grocery business in a two-storey building which now houses the O'Kane "newsagent's" shop to the left of the Cellar Bar. Partition of Ireland also saw the government mandated partition of grocery and licensed trades so the Rogers family who owned it then had to build a separate bar where the Cellar is today, at the entrance to the Shambles (salesyard). The original bar may be the one mentioned in Johnny Paul's poem as that belonging to "Patrick Rogers" because Patsy McShane tells us that Willie in the photo, his uncle, bought the spirit grocery business from Paddy Rogers, presumably of the same Rogers family. Willie had worked in the bar and shop for Rogers from he left school in 1930 until he bought it some years later. I can remember the shop in the 1950's but it was by then a chemist's shop belonging to the O'Keeney family. Mrs Angela O'Keeney was the daughter of Paddy Rogers and she would later write a pictorial history of the parish called, *Looking Back on Ballinascreen* (a valuable source for this book).

Willie's brother, John McShane (Patsy's father) managed the pub from 1962 to about 1969. An O'Kane from Swatragh (a brother of Jim O'Kane who is married to Mary O'Kane of Derrynoid and now lives in Australia) then leased it for one year and it was then sold in 1970/1971 to David O'Kane who still owns it but no longer uses the premises as he converted the cellar into the bar.

146

17. McAuley's

A traditional spirit-grocery small bar that has survived the lounge and club era. The McAuley family has been giving Ballinascreen comfort with their coal, milk and bread deliveries for a few generations and this extends into their licensed premises, "a comfortable place to take a glass in", Laughlin McNamee's mandate in a much earlier generation.

This wee pub doesn't have all the bells and whistles of the big, brash places that are now popular in Draperstown but it has a loyal clientele and a reputation among knowledgeable, local connoisseurs of being a place where you don't have to shout to be heard, a place where the craic needs neither a traditional nor a techno music soundtrack. It does have an extended back room but generally whoever is in the wee bar is part of the conversation! Barney McAuley is the genial proprietor and Deirdre, his equally genial daughter, is often behind the bar in the early evenings.

18. The Burnside Bar

Burnside on a Fair Day back in the 1930s or so. The shopfront behind the cart on the right was Thomas Quinn's bar (which became the Burnside Bar of today) but it may be further to the extreme right. (see overleaf for more BB)

Burnside Bar continued

This bar was still called Quinn's in the early 1960s. It has been known as the *Burnside* since Foncey Fullen took it over after a Mulholland family had it for some years. Foncey died in 2001 and his daughter Christine now runs the pub.

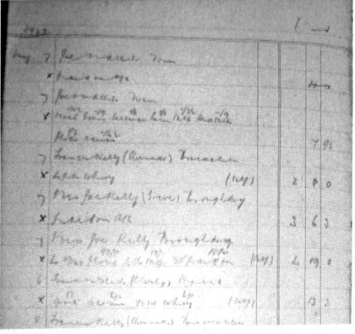

Clockwise from top left; The Burnside bar on a quiet day. Ledger from the old Thomas Quinn days.
Various artefacts including a clock that might have been made by Frank Kelly or Jim "Mickey Owen" Kelly.

It is a musical pub, very much part of the fleadhs during those banner years of 2004-2005 when the streets and bars of Draperstown were alive with music. Traditional Irish music is still played here, most recently Seamus O'Kane, Maurice Bradley and Joe Diamond getting together in 2010 for a session which was unfortunately not recorded.

The Burnside has occasional country and western groups playing along with local singers bringing a warm, rustic atmosphere to its expanded rooms which are also full of antiques and artefacts from the Quinn spirit-grocery era. You get the feeling here that it is a place very much in touch with local history. On my own last visit there, Theresa pointed out an old clock (left) that she thought was made by my father or more likely(?) by Jim "Mickey Eoghan" Kelly. She also produced a few old account ledgers from the 1920s showing sales of whiskey and other commodities to all the familiar family names in the various townlands of the parish including my own. In 1927 you could buy 3 bottles or a half-gallon of whiskey from Thomas Quinn for one pound-sixteen shillings!

After-hours drinking stories were as much a part of Thomas Quinn's as any bar in the parish. This one has been doing the rounds for many years ...

It was wartime and Pat, an inarticulate but cunning farmer, was heading home on his bicycle after a long day in the fair. It was 9:30pm and pub closing time was 9pm. Going past Quinn's at Burnside he noticed a chink of light through the curtains and he thought he would have one last drink. On opening the door he saw that there were about a dozen drinkers but the room was eerily silent. Just then he noticed the burly Draperstown police seargent in the middle of the floor writing the names of the customers in his notebook. Quick as a flash Pat looks at the barman and enquires "Sell cakes here?" Not waiting for an answer he turns on his heel and makes a quick exit!

Update: as of Sept. 2013 it looks as though The Burnside may be added to the list of "closed for good". The sign has been removed.

19. O'Donnell's
The Bar You Can Bank On
(Well maybe not at the moment. It may have closed for good in 2012.)

The Bank Bar

This was the Bank Bar during the 1930's and into Denis Kelly's time. It would not have had a big ashtray outside the door then as it does on opposite page when it became O'Donnell's. Another indication of how pubs have changed in this generation. Maybe smokers did have to step outside because I remember Denis wisely warning this errant youth one day in Portstewart, to quit the smoking because it was both unhealthy and a drain on the finances. I eventually took his advice but not for another 15 years!

the Blackthorn Bar

It became The Blackthorn Bar during the time it was owned by the Mulholland family(?) through the turn of the 21st century and more recently it was O'Donnell's. During those two eras it had to be the most noticeable bar in the town, its exterior painted in an eye-boggling bright red! (aptly enough for a post-financial-meltdown bank bar? ... in the red, needing to be bailed out?). Latest news we have on it is that it may have closed for good and is beginning to look a bit derelict.

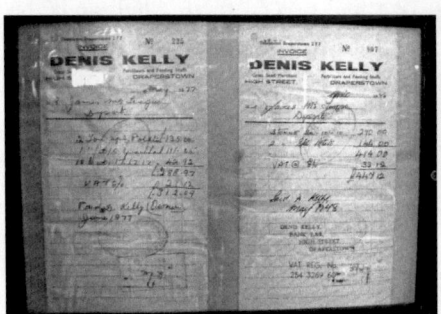

Above; Invoices from the 1960s and 70s on display in O'Donnells, a reminder of the days when Denis Kelly owned the bar and ran a business from the yard behind. Denis had a threshing machine back in the 50s too which did the rounds of farms in Ballinascreen.

Above right; a quiet day in O'Donnell's and on right, an even quieter one. Ballinabigscreen. Most bars in Ballinascreen now have a big-screen TV for their sporting customers. This photo was taken in June 2009 on F.A. Cup Final day. There were only 2 fans in the place that hot afternoon, me for Everton and a young Chelsea fan whose name I forget. He got to celebrate!

20. Mulligan's
Drumderg Draught

From here on we go rural, in the townlands surrounding Draperstown. This bar on the Moneyneena Road has changed hands a number of times in the past 50 years. In my own young days it was McCormick's. I was in it many times in my early teens in the summer of 1960 ... no, not drinking, but as an electrician's helper with Pascal Kelly who was at that time bringing electricity to many places outside of the town. I remember the "roadmen" coming in at lunch time for a bit of refreshment but was never around when the evening crowd got down to more serious tippling. The house was originally built by a James Henry. A man called Toner ran the early spirit grocer's (Toner from Brackaghdysert? a brother of the man who originally ran The Market Inn?). The sequence of owners seems to have been Felix Henry - Toners - Pat McCormick - Joe "Peter Roe" McCullagh - Seamus Mulligan - Mickey Kelly (Neilly) - Brian McGurk (he seemed to have let it out a few times) and then back to Brian Mulligan (Seamus's son).

Joe Rogers who married Pat McCormick's daughter might have had plans for this pub if the Sperrins had been able to hold on to their snow mantle on a regular basis. Joe is a well know character around the parish, an entrepreneur and master of many trades whose most ambitious project was a ski slope, complete with tractor driven ski-lift, on White Mountain out beyond Moneyneena. If it had taken off, this pub and The Hogan Stand might have done a roaring trade with the apres-ski crowd arriving from all over Ireland and beyond.

21. The Hogan Stand
From Wall Street to the Sperrins.

Only four pubs in the parish, outside of Draperstown itself, are still in operation and one of those, The Hogan Stand, in Moneyneena has been going for many years. The original pub was part of a house next door, a spirit grocer's run by the McShane family. When the law changed, the grocer's shop was moved to a tin hut across the road at the graveyard. Charles McVey (from Ballinderry) came to work in the bar and married the McShane daughter, Sarah. Then, for more than 30 years it was run by James Doyle who was a half-brother of Michael Doyle who began *The Shepherd's Rest*. In Doyle's time the pub was called **The Sperrin View**. After a fire in the old premises James Doyle built a new dwelling house and the new separate building which is the core of today's pub.

Charlie McNally, the present owner, came to Ballinascreen in 1991 from Fermanagh as did the parish priest, Fr Colm Clerkin, some years later. So the good souls of the parish depend on Fermanagh men to see them through any kind of spiritual crisis. As with the Doyles there is an American connection. Charlie worked as a barman in New York city in the financial district, where on his way to work every day in the Killarney Rose he would pass under the shadow of the World Trade Centre. In the U.S. Charlie was a keen GAA man, playing for "Leitrim" (mostly Dubliners). When he returned to Ireland and tried to buy a bar in Fermanagh but none were for sale, he searched further afield and found **The Sperrin View** in a Tyrone newspaper and bought it. His interest in the GAA was fully satisfied in 1991 in Moneyneena in which was in the midst of 5 great years for Derry football and it was a no-brainer to call his pub after the most famous football stand in Ireland especially when the best player on the Derry team was Moneyneena man, Tony Scullion, and the parish was going nuts over the success of Scullion and the rest of the team culminating in their triumphant Sam Maguire Cup win in 1993. Tony actually worked behind the Hogan Stand bar for a time.

It is probably the best sports bar in the parish with its large horseshoe shaped main bar allowing punters to watch different screens for different sports. It can accommodate over a hundred people for functions and private parties.

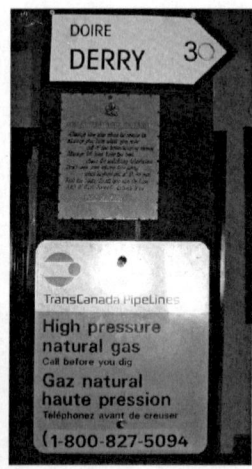

Above; Charlie McNally behind the bar at the Hogan Stand in 2009. It was packed a few nights later with local Manchester United and Barcelona fans taking in the Champions' League Final, crowding around the bar and its multiple TVs. Sign; A reminder of home for any Canadian visitors to "The Stand", a sign provided by pipeline worker, James Joseph Kennedy of Toronto, originally from Dunlogan.

Below; Local heroes, Hughie Heron, tug-of-war champion and coach from Bancran in a framed photo on a wall of The Hogan Stand and Tony Scullion at the Dublin Hogan Stand in 1993. There are many reminders of that banner year for the Derry GAA team, around the walls of Monyeneena's well-known pub.

22. The Shepherd's Rest
Community comes first.

*When the sun sets over Erin, the land St. Patrick Blessed
I'll go for recreation into The Shepherds Rest
Where the Hills of Carnanelly, in the pale moonlight they gleam
Across the great Moyola where it's just a little stream.*

from the song *The Great Moyola River*
by Gerard Conway (Glenviggan)

Not far from the old church in the Sixtowns stands one of most venerable pubs in Ireland. It has been the scene of many family gatherings including those of the "Mickey Eoghain Kellys" of Straw who have enlivened it with song and story since its opening in 1930. It probably embodies all that a community pub should. It serves the farmers of the Sixtowns but it is also a place for exiles to come home to. Along with the Corner House, the Market Bar and the Cellar Bar, it is one of Ireland's better-known pubs.

Colin Doyle (above left) runs the pub for the Doyle family who have had the premises in the family since the 13th of February 1930 (see glass door on p.157). Colin's grandfather, Michael Doyle came from Philadelphia prior to that date and bought the bar from the Bradley family who then bought 2 pubs in Coleraine where they still own one. From 1930 to 1967 the pub was simply known as "Doyle's" but on Oct 19th of '67 it was reopened after extensive renovation done by James Cleary and it was renamed "The Shepherd's Rest". The present owner, Colin's father, Michael (above right) is still very active in the day-to-day running of the pub. Michael remembers my brother Brendan Kelly doing electrical work in the bar back in the 1940s.

Because the Shepherd's Rest has hosted many a wedding, this joke might fit it better than many of the other pubs here;

At an Irish wedding reception the D.J. yelled, "Would all married men please stand next to the one person who has made your life worth living."
The bartender was almost crushed to death, but is expected to survive.

The large extended family of the Kellys of Straw have made it their celebration centre for many years and that song by Gerard Conway has been sung by many of his cousins, the children of the late Josie Conway and her "Mickey Eoghain" husband Jim Joe Kelly. On the website home page (below) for the pub the song is referred to.

From the Shepherd's Rest's own website ... http://www.shepherdsrestpub.com/

Welcome to the Shepherd's Rest

This peaceful family run pub is tucked away in the foothills of the Sperrins, where the river Moyola is just a little stream. It is an area of outstanding beauty steeped in history and folklore. The public house is at the centre of Ireland's social scene. Whether you love it, or loathe it, the pub is the hub of Irish life, and is well renowned locally for it's lively conversation, local banter and traditional wit. In the upstairs lounge you will find a cosy, relaxed atmosphere with two open fires, good music, modern and old time dancing - a popular haunt for both young and old – or you can get away from it all by having a barbecue at our fully equipped garden house, complete with hearth fire. During the winter, enjoy the craic and a good pint beside an open fire? Teas, coffee and sandwiches daily. Coach tours, private functions etc are catered for.

"The Rest" has long been associated with local song and poetry, as many pubs have been, but this one goes further by positively promoting poetry and local literature judging by the portraits in the snug above of the late "famous" Seamus Heaney and "Packy Ritchie", Paddy Richardson from Glenviggan, a life long regular in "Doyle's" until his passing in 1999, a local man with stories to tell. To reinforce this, there was a special night in 2012, to celebrate the life and words of W.F. Marshall, the poetic parson of Sixmilecross, Omagh, Co Tyrone, famous for that venerable, old verse chestnut, "Drumlister".

Local, Gerard Conway is also celebrated here (below left) with a portrait and handwritten copy of the much-loved song *The Great Moyola River* which he penned, paying homage to the Shepherd's Rest itself. Below right is the etched glass door commemorating the "Doyle's" gentleman founder.

The Shepherd's Rest in beautiful Moyard

23. St Colm's GAA

Latecomer (opened in 1995) to the wine and spirit trade around Ballinascreen but probably doing better business than most of the older pubs. Around feiseanna, football and funerals this place is frequently full. The stage next door hosts performers from all over.

24. McAllister's

Drinking Straw Style

The only pub in the village/townland of Straw for the last 60 years since Miles's closed and one which this editor knows better than any other pub in the parish so it has to get the full treatment here! He lived in it! When I go into the bar end of McAllister's, not the lounge end, for a pint these days, (once every few years) I always let somebody know, whether they want to hear it or not, that we are now sitting in what used to be our kitchen/living room and hallway. When our family came back from Canada in 1952 we rented the row house between what was then McAllister's small bar and Charlie and Kate Donnelly's similar house. (see 40s-50s photo below). We left in 1957. In the early 1970's the first floor of "our" house was gutted and renovated to become the present bar.

Back in those early 1950s the bar seemed a busy place. There might be drinkers around our door or out back afterhours in the shed (1950s style patio!) behind our house. On Fair Days the drinking, guldering and singing ringing out from the shed would go on well into the Saturday morning. It didn't bother us children but I'm sure it was hard on our parents who didn't drink. In those days before TV, McAllisters was our soap opera, horse opera, sitcom, reality show, horror show, documentary and variety show all rolled into one. There was rarely a dull day or night around the place, the farm, the shop and the bar all providing gritty entertainment. What follows is partly my own reminiscences but mostly that of the late Joseph McAllister, brother of the present owner of the pub, Peter.

The original small spirit grocery and dwelling house were what is in the 1950s photo the one storey shed on the right of the main building, a very modest affair indeed compared to the fairly large building today. It had a door and windows looking out on the main road and was probably thatched. In Joseph's young day (and mine) it was a storage shed for meal and corn and still had the door, always barred, out onto the street. At the corner of Comhrac Road there was a large stone on the ground, built into the structure to stop turning carts hitting the corner of the building. Joseph thought the earliest known owners were McKeowns. In the early 1900s Felix O'Neill and his brother Barney acquired it. Felix worked down at Donnelly's flax mill on the Milltown Road but was injured in an accident there, losing an arm. With the 60 pounds compensation he received he bought the spirit grocery and farm from the McKeowns. Felix married an aunt of recently desceased James McBride of Strawmore but they had no children so when Felix died he left the business to his nephew Johnny McAllister, Joseph's father, who began to operate the spirit grocery and farm around 1924-5 when he was almost in his 50th year. He had the present structure built which has gone through many changes over the years but has kept its general shape.

It is the only business left in Straw since Joe Coyle's shop closed its doors in the 1960s and it would have to be considered, in its heyday, the commercial hub of Straw, Strawmore, Comhrac, Díseart and beyond. Since the advent of Draperstown supermarkets the shop lost much of its trade and wouldn't rate as more than a "convenience store" today but the pub has managed to maintain customers in large part through the efforts over the years to keep it up-to-date in a changing pub landscape. All the pubs in the parish would have adapted more or less successfully, or not at all, to the changing times and many of them would have similar characteristics to McAllisters especially those in the rural townlands.

Back in the 1950s and 60s McAllister's bar had a clientele of characters well known around Ballinascreen, many of them farmers, cattle dealers, and friends of owner Johnny's. Drinking would begin in the bar but that would close at 9 p.m. and drinkers would then retire to the 1950s version of "the patio" (the Paddy-O?), in other words anywhere in the adjoining buildings and yards which were all part of the licensed premises but the local constabulary would have little tolerance for drink being sold beyond the closing time.

In 1962 (above) Johnny McAllister's name was still on the sign but that along with the monkey puzzle tree, the Regent petrol sign and the garden wall are all gone now. I can remember sitting on the step on the extreme right, in the shade, on a hot days in the late 1950s. About 5-6 years before this the petrol tanks had been buried in the garden behind the low wall and the pumps themselves were hand-operated lever jobs. Below; more changes in the late 1960s.

You could take bottles home of course but in those days that was not the norm so once again the laws got bent a bit. Joe "Crig" Bradley (above) who was barman, shopkeeper and all round manager of the place, could be seen out on the front street after 9 o'clock looking up and down the road to see if the constabulary was abroad before resuming his serving or running to warn the boyos in the stable or the schoolyard or the back sheds to make themselves scarce. Afterhours drinking was carried on in any number of bars in the parish and its illicit nature always added a bit of ambience to the proceedings i.e. the crack was often better even if half the time the conversation had to be whispered.

Part of the McAllister buildings was a small, disused stable just around the Comhrac Road corner which was a favoured afterhours drinking spot. We schoolkids played in it at lunch time now and again, shooting pellets at targets on one of the stall posts. The floor seemed to be turf mold which was soft and probably lent a bit of warmth to the drinkers who sat in there of a cold winter night looking out at their ancestors' gravestones beyond the wall of the old graveyard on the other side of the road, like the towering Carleton plot archangel on the left. Maybe no Carletons drank in the stable but plenty of O'Hagans, Kellys, and O'Neills would have moved their kindred spirits over the wall and none other than Laughlin McNamee himself, interred in plot No. 25, next to the chapel, would have smiled in his grave at the thought of tipplers so near.

McAllisters' warm kitchen would have been the preferred location but this would be more for Johnny's closer friends. I can remember being sent for some grocery item to the shop in the evening and having to knock at the kitchen door to get someone to serve me, seeing into the kitchen where an assortment of patrons would be sitting around the stove and table drinking, smoking and chatting amiably enough while Pauline, Johnny's wife, moved among them doing kitchen chores, or the young McAllisters running in and out along with furtive hens, sleepy dogs and, during pigging time, the odd pet pig nosing around the hearth. On some evenings there might have been an edge to the atmosphere especially on Fair Days when the drinking might have been a bit more excessive and old rivalries would emerge.

This is in no way meant as an insult to the McAllisters. After all it is supposed to be *Mrs Kelly's* kitchen! The illustration on the right may be of the stereotypical "pigs in the Irish kitchen" variety but Alexy Pendle's illustration of Mrs Kelly's kitchen in Anthony Trollope's 19th century novel *The Kellys and The O'Kellys* is close. Take away some of the anachronisms and stereotypes and you have something a wee bit like the view from the front hall into McAllister's kitchen of the 1950s. There were no floor-sitters, bare feet or long beards in the 1950s but it conveys a similar feeling of warmth and contentment about the hearth for animals and humans that was evident in that Straw kitchen.

Joseph remembered 1950"s-60s regulars like Jim "The Jowel" (from "jewel" ... something to do with his early days in Belfast?) in need of sustenance, "rescuing" chicken from a pot on the stove, Tommy Hagan with his sharp wit, Jim "The Navvy" Devlin, salmon poacher, Mickey Heron, Johnny Doherty who worked at Mick Crilly's mill (previously our Kelly's mill), Jim Mullan and his brother Fran who was barman there at one time, "Tom Bottles" and "Guyler", a character I was to run into later while serving him in Cuskeran's Moyola Bar. Matt Cuskeran (before owning his own bar) provided the entertainment manys a night with his marvellous singing. He was a member of the chapel choir for many years but in McAllisters he was known for his great renditions of Al Jolson songs and as Joseph put it, "He didn't have to be asked."

A few regulars were hardened drinkers who went beyond the standard fare of Guinness stout and whiskey naggin. Joseph remembered one meths drinker around the bar and yard whose urine smelled like cat's pee, a reminder of the days of meths and ether drinking that Draperstown was notorious for a century earlier.

Patrick Oliver Kelly was also a regular visitor to the bar but he did not partake of the 'dreaded alcohol'. Sometimes the "Sweeneys" would arrive, 10 -15 cartloads of "travelling people", necessitating a lockdown of shop, bar and house. It was no joke having to contend with this invasion which could be frightening for all concerned. Sheer numbers could overrun the premises, begging, demanding, stealing, trying to get in where they could.

The bar wouldn't necessarily be open during "opening hours". Keeper of the keys, Joe Crig, might be working at other tasks and would have to be found if a few customers showed up during a quiet day. Times could be hard during winter months. Farmers couldn't afford whiskey so "Two 'touts for two louts!" would be the call. Guinness was the staple, bottled on the premises from kegs or hogsheads. A keg (paid for in advance to Guinness) could fill 22 dozen bottles, each bottle sold at a shilling apiece. Fair days would bring many extra customers from far flung townlands and things could get rough. Townland rivalries were strong and old battles not forgotten. Sixtowns people might not get along with Comhrac people. Strawmore men might not be too fond of Doonmen. This was evident even among kids at the local school but when the "oul boys" got into the drink there was always a chance of fights breaking out, more grappling and "shovin and rasslin" than any real fisticuffs. There might be Sinn Feiners mixing it up with Hibernians. What divisions were the cause of this tragic fight mentioned in the 1836 Ordnance Survey memoir?

"John Toner, farmer, was killed in the year 1834 by Philip Kelly, farmer. They both lived in the townland of Straw. The cause was a drinking dispute. The murderer absconded and fled to America."

We don't know of any such drastic disputes around McAllisters in the last century but who knows what old, deep-rooted family vendettas haunted and provoked the drinkers around Straw right into the years that my generation knew?

In 1961 Johnny McAllister died and his wife Pauline took over the business. Her name appears on the sign in the 1969 photo (p. 161) and other changes were now visible. The garden wall is gone. Soon the small pub behind the pumps would be expanded to include the house on the left and by the early 1970's a lounge would take over the shop on the right and extend well back through the old building and beyond. This would have been typical of many Irish pubs at the time. Lounge it or lose it.

All through the 1950s to the late 60s Joe "Crig" Bradley ran the pub as already mentioned. How many Bradleys is that we have encountered, so far, in the bar business? He began there at the age of 14 and was a fixture of the village for a generation. Gerry McAllister took over the pub after his mother died and in the early 1970's he and brother Joseph did major renovations.

Classic Straw photo of Joseph McAllister, Anne Gallagher and Vera O'Kane on McAllisters' front yard sometime in the mid- to late 1960's. The venerable, vintage Austin 7 was Willie Costello's of Strawmore. Frank Kelly's house is on the left (by then the curate's parochial house). Donaghy's house is on the right beyond the walled Donnelly front garden with its distinctive Straw landmark monkey puzzle tree (Araucaria araucana) dwarfing the Regent petrol sign.

Joseph added the large lounge before running the pub himself in 1975-6. Joseph brought big changes with music groups and "Take Your Pick" games which drew the crowds from Friday to Monday. Nobody ever won "the trip to Tenerife" but one lady did win the weekend trip to Dublin. This entertainment was breaking new ground for Ballinascreen pubs. "Barnbrack" from Derry was one of popular music groups that played McAllisters and the leader of the band usually doubled as the M.C. of the game show. "A wild time." Joseph said, although the real heyday of the pub would have been '73 to '75. A growing economy in Draperstown, EU subsidies, plenty of money, drink flowing freely, everybody buying rounds. They would have hired part-time staff to cope with the crowds unlike the old days when somebody working out in the fields would have had the key of the closed bar in their pocket and would have had to be fetched to open up for a customer or two.

Things are quieter again today. Drinking habits have changed. As of 2009 there was but one regular Guinness drinking customer in McAllisters (no draft Guinness on tap) so that staple of the old pub is almost a memory.

There you have it, the last of a "two-four" of pubs in Ballinascreen but the very last words are left to a Bard of the Bar, one Tommy Keenan of Strawmore ...

Gerry McAllister in 1972. The new shop is at the far end, the petrol pumps moved out from the building, his mother's name still on the sign and the marks of years of bicycle leaning still on the wall below the window of the old shop.

A Bard of the Bar
Thomas the Rhymer

    Below is a poem Gerry McAllister came across - he remembered Mick O'Neill (the Bing) used to recite it in the bar (McAllister's). It was sent in a letter from America, by a fellow called Tommy Keenan who used to live in Tonagh Lane (now River Road/Strawmore - as you go round to Paddy McGlade's) Tommy's father came from elsewhere to work in Kelly's mill and he had been known as "Miller Keenan." Tommy went to America later and wrote this poem to his friend Mick O'Neill.

    When Straw or other Ballinascreen emigrants to the New York area during the 1930s-60s, were looking for work, some would have found their way to Tommy Keenan's home in Beacon on the Hudson, about 70 miles north of NY City. He never forgot his friends and neighbours from Straw and helped them get used to their new country, sponsoring at least one of them. Some would have found work at the local Beacon asylum which was part of a correctional facility. This kind of work was common back then for young Irish people just starting out. One ex-Straw man who lived closer to NY City and who was a friend and frequent visitor of Tommy's used to say that he could remember everything about Ballinascreen just the way it was when he left. Obviously Tommy Keenan remembered it well too and wrote these verses.

From Tommy Keenan to Mick "The Bing" O'Neill.

On looking back for forty years
Through skies that are turning grey
My memory asks me to record
Some hardships of our day,
But also many joyful things
From memory I can draw,
Amongst them is the faithful friends
I had in dear old Straw.

I know it's not a city great,
Nor even yet a town,
But nowhere else in Ireland
More faithful friends are found.
For me that spent my early life
Not far from Kelly's Mill
To walk again over Myles's bridge
Would my last wish fulfill.

I remember Sunday mornings well
When we went to holy Mass,
We'd stand around the graveyard
To watch the people pass
And when they rang the final bell
To call us to our prayers
We'd far too often slither in
And kneel upon the stairs.

And nearly always after Mass
To your house we would go.
Your mother dear, God rest her soul,
Is in heaven now I know.
She'd always link the kettle
I can hear her voice today.
"Sit over here my, Tommy boy
and take this drop of tay."

And then across the river
And head for home again,
To walk around by Barney's dam
When we lived in Tonagh Lane
and then I'd have some dinner,
Though it wasn't chops and steak,
And again we'd meet on Tommy's street
Our evening plans to make.

I would sit and wait for Eddie there
And Joe Pat Matha too,
And maybe if you had to shave
We all would wait on you.
The bikes we had were not so good
But we knew the faults they'd got
And if the brakes refused to work
We would brake them with our foot.

We sang and danced for miles around
No place seemed far away,
And glad were we when taken down
To get a cup of tea.
We sang and danced from Cranagh
Away down to Gortahurk,
And paid the price on Monday
When we had to go to work.

We did our part for freedom too
When few saw things our way,
And stood on guard on stormy nights
And worked hard all next day.
We walked to Sperrin with tender feet,
From shoes that needed soles,
And slept up on the County March
Behind the rocks in holes.

Enough is said of all the things
That you and I have done.
Though some was for the rights of man
And some was just for fun.
And some to ask God for his grace
To light our darkened way,
As all alone we're trudging home
On that last and final day.

We've seen the Cleary's in July,
They both are looking well.
Their family is the finest
Which is not hard to tell.
Johnnie is retired now
And smokes his pipe all day.
And Martha laughs as hearty
As she did on Dysart bray.

Now Maggie Ann sends her regards
And prays that Father Time
Will roll the years so gently on
That to you he will be kind.
And though my family you don't know
The wish for me to send
A wish of health and happiness
To their father's boyhood friend.

I regret to close this letter, Mick
But there's little else to say,
But wish that I could walk out now
And stroll down Shibby's bray
And we could sit on old Straw Road
Along the graveyard wall,
We'd talk of things of long ago
What stories we'd recall.

Bibulous Bibliography

Berresford-Ellis, Peter; *The Druids*. Eerdmans Pub Co; Grand Rapids, Michigan, Reprint Edition (June 1995)
Carroll, Sean; *From Eternity to Here*. New York, Dutton/Penguin, 2010.
Carson, Ciaran; *Shamrock Tea*. London, Granta Books 2002.
Carson, Ciaran; *The Táin*. London, Penguin Classics, 2007.
Cohen, Leonard; *Stranger Music*. Toronto, McClelland and Stewart, 1993.
Connell, K. H.; "Ether-Drinking in Ulster" from *Irish Peasant Society; Four Historical Essays*, Oxford, Clarendon Press, 1968.
Coulter, Rev. J. A.; *Ballinascreen*. Derry Diocese(?) 1953.
Curl, James Stevens; *Moneymore and Draperstown*. Ulster Architectural Heritage Society, 1979.
Hart, Ernest; "Ether Drinking", essay reprinted in *Looking Back on Ballinascreen* by Angela O'Keeney, B. H. S., 1989.
Hepburn, David; *The Kaylie*. London, Houlston & Sons, 1884. Republished by Moyola Books, Labby, Ireland, 1994.
Heaney, Seamus; most of his books.
Hutton, Ronald; *The Druids*. Hambledon Continuum; 1st edition (May 1, 2007)
Logan, William Bryant; *Oak: The Frame of Civilization*, New York, WW Norton and Co, 2005.
Longley, Michael; *Poems 1963 - 1983*. London, Secker and Warburg, 1991.
Macalister, R. A. Stewart; *The Secret Languages of Ireland*. Cambridge University Press, 1937. Facsimile edition published by Craobh Rua Books, Armagh, Ireland, 1997.
McGovern, Patrick E.; *Uncorking the Past*. Berkely and Los Angeles, University of California Press, 2009.
O Canainn, Aodh; *Teacht Den tSliabh Trathnona*. Binn Eadair (Howth), Cosceim, 2000.
O'Kane, James; *The Bard of Carntogher*. Broc Press, Portsmouth, 1982.

The following are all Ballinascreen Historical Society (B. H. S.) books, most of them written, edited or compiled by Graham Mawhinney.

Deery, Fr. Leo; *The Schools of Ballinascreen*.
Harkin, Hugh; *The Life and Adventures of Hudy McGuigan*, 1841. Reprint 1993.
Kelly, John 'Paul'; *In Crockmore's Shade*. 1991.
O'Keeney, Angela J.; *Looking Back on Ballinascreen*, 1989.
Ordnance Survey Memoir for the Parish of Ballinascreen (1836-1837) pub. 1981.
A Century Makes Changes; The South Derry and District Almanac (1902/1909). pub. 2000.
The Wee Black Tin; Poems of John Kelly and George Barnett. pub. 1980
Ballinascreen Gravestone Inscriptions; Straw "old" graveyard, 2008.
John O'Donovan's Letters from County Londonderry (1834). pub. 1992.

Photograph credits; Shane Kelly, Isabelle Hegarty, Sheena & Pat Bradley, Anne McAlister, Steven Noonan (for the late Paddy Heron's collection), Patsy McShane, Graham Mawhinney, Michael McNamee, Corbis Images, Hubble telescope website, Google map site, Moore Group site, Wikipedia site. Many of the postcard images used were the work of Graham Mawhinney's granduncle, Alfred W. McWhinney (the surname spelling changed back and forth over the generations). He had an early 20th century photographic studio at Kilcronaghan.

JOHNNY'S AMUSEMENTS

An Bothar Buí

PREVIOUS BALLINASCREEN HISTORICAL SOCIETY PUBLICATIONS

Orders from outside U.K. please add 20% to cover postage. Only Sterling draft cheques payable to Ballinascreen Historical Society.
All orders / enquires to:- Ballinascreen Historical Society, C/O 5 Tobermore Road, Draperstown Co. Londonderry, N. Ireland, BT45 7AG

1980	'The Wee Black Tin' (Poems by George Barnett and John 'Paul' Kelly)	out of print
1981	'Ordnance Survey Memoir for Ballinascreen 1836-37'	out of print
1982	'The Meetin House' (Draperstown Presbyterian Church History)	out of print
1983	'Statistical Reports of Six Derry Parishes, 1821' (Ballinascreen, Kilcronaghan, Desertmartin, Boveva, Banagher, Dungiven)	out of print
1984	'Songs and Music of Ballinascreen' (L.P. record & cassette)	sold out
1985	'Notes on the Place names of Parishes and Townlands of the county of Londonderry' by A. M. Munn, 1925 (Limited edition reprint)	out of print
1986	'Ordnance Survey Memoirs for the Parishes of Desertmartin and Kilcronaghan, 1836-1837'	out of print
1986	'Images of Ballinascreen' – V.H.S. video cassette	sold out
1987	'Famous Maghera Men' by Eoin Walsh	out of print
1988	'The Heart of Ballinascreen' – Poems by - Nora Ni Chathain	out of print
1989	'Looking Back on Ballinascreen' – A miscellany of writings relating to the district	out of print
1990	'The Autobiography of Thomas Witherow, 1824-1890'	£8.95 inc. p&p
1991	'In Crockmore's Shade' – A selection of poems by John 'Paul' Kelly (1884-1944) of Doon, Draperstown	£3.50 inc. p&p
1992	'John O'Donovan's letters from County Londonderry (1834)' – letters containing information collected during the progress of the Ordnance Survey	out of print
1993	'The Life and Adventures of Hudy McGuigan' - by Hugh Harkin	£5.50 inc. p&p
1994	'Gleanings from Ulster History' by Seamus O'Ceallaigh (1879-1954)	out of print
1995	'Griffith's Valuation (1859) – Magherafelt Union'	out of print
1996	'The Big House – Derrynoyd Lodge, Draperstown' - Notes on the Torrens/O'Neill family and their former home, now site of The Rural College	out of print
1996	'The McHenry Letters (1834-46)' – Correspondence from Rev. J. L. McHenry of Culdaff, Co. Donegal to his mother at Owenreagh, Draperstown	out of print
1997	'A Hospital at Magherafelt' Part 1 – The Workhouse and Famine times in South Derry	
1998	'A Hospital at Magherafelt' - Part 2 – The Workhouse – the final fifty years (1891-1941)	
	both parts 1 and 2 out of print	
1998	'A Hospital at Magherafelt' Part 3 – The Hospital years – from 1941	£7.75 inc. p&p
1999	'Lewis's Loughinsholin (1837)' – South Derry extracts from Samuel Lewis's Topographical Dictionary of Ireland	£5.60 inc. p&p
2000	'A Century makes Changes' – Selected extracts from the South Derry & District Almanac 1902/1909	£5.00 inc. p&p
2001	'Shaw Mason's Maghera (1814) and Killelagh (1819)'	£3.50 inc. p&p
2002	'Change and Decay' – Bygone Buildings of Ballinascreen	out of print
2003	'The Churches of Ballinascreen' - A set of nine postcards	£4.00 inc. p&p
2003	'Ballinascreen' by Mgr. J A Coulter (1919-1983)	£7.50 inc. p&p
2004	'Memorial Inscriptions' – St Columba's & St Anne's	out of print
2005	"Those were the days!" by Owen Kelly	out of print
2006	"A Generation of Montgomerys" by Rt. Rev. Bishop Henry Montgomery (1847-1932)	£5.75 inc p&p
2007	"The Schools of Ballinascreen (1823 - 1990)" by Fr. Leo Deery, P.P."	out of print
2008	"Ballinascreen Gravestone Inscriptions - Straw Old graveyard	out of print
2009	"Ballinascreen Gravestone Inscriptions - Moneynena Old Graveyard"	£5.00 inc p&p
2010	"Ballinascreen Gravestone Inscriptions - Old Church, Moneyconey & St. Patrick's Church, Tullybrick"	£5.00 inc p&p
2011	"Kilcronaghan Gravestone Inscriptions - Old Church, Mormeal & Presbyterian Church, Tobermore"	£5.00 inc p&p
2012	"Far From Ballinascreen" by John McHugh	£11.00 inc p&p

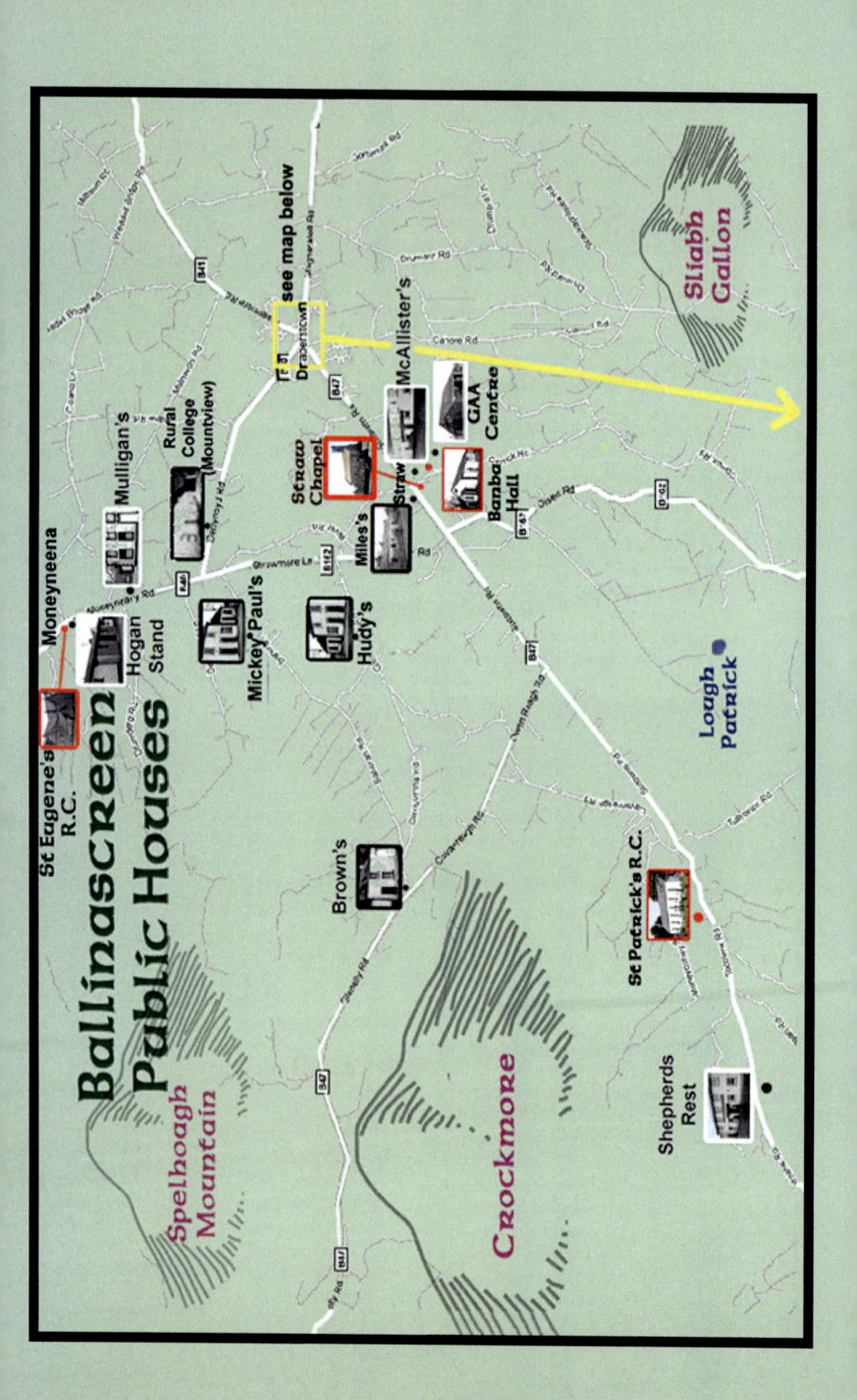

Ballinascreen Public Houses

- St Eugene's R.C. — Moneyneena
- Mulligan's
- Rural College (Mountview)
- Hogan Stand
- Straco Chapel
- McAllister's
- Straw
- GAA Centre
- Banba Hall
- Miles's
- Mickey Paul's
- Hudy's
- Brown's
- St Patrick's R.C.
- Shepherds Rest

Spelboagh Mountain
Crockmore
Sliabh Gallon
Lough Patrick
Draperstown (see map below)